And Then The Snow Fell

Vikki Hammond

Dedication

For Kai. For teaching me all I know. For showing me a love I never thought was possible, a love so fierce and pure. For teaching everyone you came across what a special, amazing boy you were. For being so brave, sometimes for the both of us. For giving me 15 wonderful years that I will treasure forever, and for living life as hard as you did. I love you always. Until we are together again. x

For Bailey, Honey-Mae, Daisy and Lola for being amazing children and making me proud every single day. x

Acknowledgements

Kirsty Moseley, yet again going out of your way to help me put our story into a book.

Katie Stead, for proof reading my books.

Hilda Reyes, for designing my cover exactly how I wanted it.

A Note From The Editor

With kind permission of Vikki, I wanted to add a few words of my own. This is the final chapter in Kai's story. I feel so privileged to have proof read all three books for Vikki, and I hope I have done them justice.

Vikki's story of bringing Kai into the world and raising him as best she can, despite all the obstacles in her way, is truly inspiring. She is an amazing woman who fought to the bitter end to ensure Kai had everything he ever needed.

When I was first introduced to you through Kirsty I didn't know your story, but through reading these books for you your story is now forever etched in my heart.

Stay strong forever Queen Vikki, your King will be waiting for you when your time is ready.

Love and strength to you always.

Katie xx

Author's Note

Some names have been changed to protect people's identities.

RECOVERY
2015/16

Looking after a very poorly child is hard at the best of times, but to be left with no support was bloody frightening.

After Kai came home from Great Ormond Street hospital, I thought we would be inundated with appointments, support and someone to contact for advice.

The reality was me home alone with Kai constantly worrying if he was healing well, if his bowels were opening enough and trying to teach him to walk again.

Kai had been rushed into surgery after a very serious bowel blockage which then caused him to have a cardiac arrest, sepsis and septic shock. We got told so many times that Kai wouldn't make it and asked if we wanted to turn off his life support machine. We refused, and after a whole month on life support we finally had our boy home where he belonged.

We later found out that Kai's event could have been due to the drugs trial he was on. Everolimus, a cancer drug, showed signs of helping those with Tuberous Sclerosis Complex. The drug showed signs of shrinking tumours that Kai's little organs were riddled with. His heart, kidneys and brain had so many tumours. His seizures were also very bad and there was evidence to show that this drug helped.

We spent months getting up at 5am every Monday to travel to Addenbrookes hospital. We were not told if the drug was a placebo or the actual drug itself. We were to record all his seizures in a diary. His weight, blood pressure and bloods were done every week to make sure he was OK.

The drug trial was not something we had taken lightly. We read up on it as much as we could, discussing the pros and cons. As it was a drug trial we were putting Kai onto something that had very little information with regards to TSC patients. We were running out of options, and watching Kai having so many seizures helped us with our decision.

At the time I really thought this could be the answer and Kai would be able to continue the drug after the trial ended. Unfortunately, after Kai's bowel blockage Dr James, Scott and I agreed that we couldn't risk him going through something so dangerous again.

The drug has done wonders for other patients, but for Kai it nearly cost him his life. The side effects aren't well known. Kai didn't have the usual ones such as mouth ulcers - he had become very constipated, which when I pointed out to professionals was met with sachets of Movicol. This didn't shift the hard lumps, it just caused the overflow to go around. I felt such guilt that I had put him on a drug that had caused his bowels to become impacted. There really was no other option and, unfortunately, Kai was unlucky. I know many others to which this drug has been a life saver.

We were told Kai would need regular appointments at Great Ormond Street Hospital, as well as home visits from the community nurses and a local support team.

As the weeks and months went by we had none of this, the physio team only came twice. They showed us how to strengthen his legs and gave us a support belt to assist when he could stand up. Kai could barely stand at this point, it was like having a baby all over again, a 5-foot-tall baby!

Kai had lost so much weight he looked and was classed as malnourished. It was a constant cycle of giving him high fat foods, lots of snacks and fluids and then worrying if he could go to the toilet after. Touch wood his bowels after the operation were better and he was filling his nappy up as he should.

Throughout this period, we were sleeping alongside Kai in his room as we were worried in case he needed us or filled his nappy during the night. When Scott went back to work it was hard for those few months being housebound with a child as big as Kai. I cherished every moment together though, knowing he would soon be back to school and I would be worried sick about leaving him.

Over time, Kai was able to sit up, that moved from sliding off the sofa and scooting across the carpet on his long 'bambi legs' as I called them. He was so chuffed that he was able to move about and I can't take any of the praise as it was all him. Sheer determination and strength on his part, Scott and I often said if that was us we would be bed bound for months after. Not Kai he wanted to be back up and causing mischief as soon as he could!

It wasn't long before he was trying to stand up alone, which very nearly sent me grey. If I left the room I would hear a bang and come back to find him on the floor smiling. He was so determined that Scott had no choice but to hold him up and walk him up and down the room every night until he got it all out of his system.

Around six weeks after his operation Kai was walking with Scott when he shrugged him off and walked alone, very unsteady but alone. His little face beamed, and he shouted, "Mum, Mum." We were all cheering and laughing and managed to get it on video. Nothing kept our boy down for long!

With no sign of a follow-up appointment, I was chasing the hospital daily. I felt angry that we were forgotten about with no concrete plan in place for a child as poorly as Kai was. It took a lot of shouting, screaming and threatening to finally get our appointments through.

They were pleased with Kai and couldn't believe how a child so close to death was now happy and walking about as if nothing had happened. In fact, the only reminder, physically, for us was his scar running up his tummy and the weight loss. We started

4

to increase his milkshakes to 2-3 sachets a day adding double cream and full fat milk into them.

Trying to get weight onto someone is harder than it sounds. Especially as someone as active as Kai! Even if he was sitting on the sofa Kai would be rocking away and bouncing up and down. I would sit and wonder how many calories he was burning off after all my effort!

Three months after coming off life support Kai went back to school, he was so happy sitting in his wheelchair waiting for his school bus to come. I was sat in floods of tears worrying about the phone ringing with another message to meet them at the hospital like before. His school were amazing and kept in constant contact with me. They were equally as nervous as I was, knowing that so much could change in an instant with Kai as we had seen months previously.

I was so happy to have Kai home where he belonged, but mentally my mind had taken a battering. Night times, again, were the worst and panic had started to seep out of every pore. I was obsessed even more so with Kai and what could go wrong next. A slight worry would build up in my head and flow out in a horrid built up panic. My heart would race then slow right down until I was convinced it would stop at any moment. I would shake and tremble, have flash backs of Kai wired up to all those machines, and my kids crying down the phone at me to come home.

It got to a point where I was driving myself mad and Scott, Beckie and Terri told me to go to the Doctor. I felt horrid, everyone could see Kai was now home, back to school, walking and gaining weight. I felt like screaming that this wasn't the end, I was still terrified inside and all the responsibility of looking after Kai was on my shoulders. What if I missed that he hadn't opened his bowels today? What if he had opened his bowels and it wasn't enough? Had I given him enough calories today? I felt horrid taking Kai out so obviously underweight as I felt people would think I wasn't doing my best for my son.

I took everyone's advice and went to see the Doctor. He was amazing and listened to how I felt, listened to my explanation of flash backs, panic, dread and not sleeping. He diagnosed me with post-traumatic stress disorder and depression.

It sounds silly to say but I felt like I had let myself and everyone down. Here I was at home with my family and everything I ever wanted in life. Children, a loyal husband, a home, our own business and I still couldn't be happy. Why, after Kai was home and, on the mend, was I sinking into a fog of depression again? I hadn't felt low like that in years and struggled to understand how a mum of five could be diagnosed with PTSD. At that time, I thought it was what only soldiers got! The doctor prescribed some anti-depressants and put me on the list for counselling, which I knew I needed more than tablets. The tablets I put in my cupboard and they stayed there; I was never any good with trying medication!

The months rolled past, and as well as dealing with my children's emotions I had started to deal with mine. The girls were especially worried every time Kai had a hospital appointment. Daisy would sob and cry and beg me not to go as she was worried I would not come back, like in February when I told them I wouldn't be long and ended up staying in Great Ormond Street Hospital for over a month. I often felt guilt over the things my children had seen in their short lives. Lola, for instance, knew from around 18 months how to deal with a seizure. She would push toys out of the way and get Kai's mat for me to lay him on. Honey-Mae is very like me, she will put on a brave face and smile when inside she feels anything but happy. Daisy is the sensitive one and can cry at adverts (she gets that from her Dad!) and Bailey will go off to his room and work out his emotions alone.

I had started to feel a bit more in control of the panic and felt happier that I had shared with someone how low I was feeling. Of course, the flashbacks and panic were still there, but with every day it got a little easier to cope with.

The months flew by, Kai was gaining weight which was a big relief as I had become obsessed with it. Dietician input had been organised by Dr James which was an immense help, but there were still very few follow-ups regarding Kai's bowel which worried me a lot. Surely a child that had been as poorly as Kai and still had on going issues with their bowels should be monitored closely with regular check-ups?

I could not understand it, and as self-pitying as it sounds I was fed up of my child always being forgotten about. Every single thing was a fight. It was exhausting constantly chasing appointments and results, medication and equipment, or an explanation for the lack of it! I couldn't understand how some families had so much help and support yet we, like many others, had none.

Sometimes Kai struggled to open his bowels and I would try everything from massaging his tummy, warm baths, hot drinks and laxatives. He was still having Movicol and suppositories but sometimes he would still strain going to the toilet.

I wasn't told how much he should be going or how regularly, there was no plan of action in place, no after-care and no one who seemed to give a shit! Beckie would help me sit him on the toilet and we would raise his legs up and sit for over an hour sometimes waiting for him to go. He would push and strain and sometimes we were lucky, then we would be dancing around the bathroom singing and cheering while as Kai sat bemused.

We still had plenty of other appointments to attend - Kai had an appointment for nearly every single organ in his body. Heart, eyes, brain, kidneys, spine and feet to name a few. He had now been diagnosed with Scoliosis of the spine, which is where the spine curves from side to side, this can be very dangerous in severe cases but luckily his was mild. He was also very flat footed, and his feet turned inwards slightly, another reason why we called him 'Bambi legs'.

Kai had a very distinctive walk, it was so cute, he would slightly hunch over and would almost gallop his steps. We also found out around this time that Kai's kidney tumours had grown quite quickly, this was a huge worry to us kidneys problems with TSC can be very complicated, and in some cases can be life threatening. Although not big enough to cause a concern, the rate they had grown in a year was enough to worry us all. It was thought that coming off the drug trial had allowed his kidney tumours start to grow again.

One of the very reasons we wanted Kai on the trial was to help with his seizures, but also to shrink his brain tumours and stop his kidney tumours from becoming a big threat to him. Now he was off the drug there was nothing stopping them picking up the pace and continuing as they did before. I felt sick, I couldn't let him back on the drug due to the severe side effects he had from it, but now he was even more at risk.

That is the sick thing with TSC - it is so unpredictable and as soon as you think you have one issue under control another problem arises. We were also told that Kai now had new cysts on his kidneys, which again can cause problems later if they get to a big enough size, as they can interfere with kidney function and/or cause a kidney bleed. We didn't know what to make of this; it was positive they still were far away from causing him problems now, but what about the future?

Kai's heart was also a concern as from the cardiac arrest they were monitoring him yearly. We were sent a little box to monitor his heart overnight, which I was adamant he wouldn't keep on, but Kai being Kai always liked to prove me wrong and he kept it on the whole time! This then had to be sent back to the hospital through the post and they would give you the results a week later.

Of course, it didn't happen like that and I was chasing results for a few weeks after. They found that Kai had a few ectopic beats in the night which sent my anxiety through the roof. We were told that they weren't concerned by this result as Kai was very active with his movements. It showed his seizures which they expected, but still it doesn't stop the worrying.

A YEAR TO THE DAY

Christmas was fast approaching and after the worst year ever I was so excited! I never thought I would get another Christmas with Kai after him being on life support, and we were determined to make the best one yet! My step mum, Terri, had now moved up from London to be closer to us, along with my brother, Harry, and my sister, Lily-Rose.

We had never spent a Christmas together before, so we decided that this year we would, after all we had so much to celebrate! My sister, Georgia, and Scott's Auntie Sheila, were also going to be spending Christmas with us, so there would be 13 of us in total all at my house. I couldn't wait and did a huge food shop, two huge bags of potatoes, a massive turkey and so many vegetables the kids all groaned! I filled up two trollies worth of food and all the things you deprive yourself of for the entire year, or never usually buy, but suddenly decide that you now need them for this one day!

We decorated the house and put up the tree, which Kai hadn't really bothered with since he was very little, now suddenly he couldn't keep his hands off it! We couldn't have the chocolates in wrappers hanging anymore as he now knew what these were and would get up and help himself to them, wrappers still attached! Every time I left the room he would spring up and give the tree a slap, or run a Kai shaped hole into it.

Every Christmas eve it was our tradition that Beckie comes over with Jude, her son, and we would open our presents from each other and have a McDonald's. We have done this since Kai was two years old, and of course it couldn't be any other takeaway but a 'Magic M' as we called it.

Christmas came, and we had a lovely day. The children got everything they asked for and more; they had all been through so much I wanted this to be a Christmas to remember!

The tree was a sorry state, the balls had the glitter sucked off them by Lola and Kai, the tinsel was looking bare and there were so many Kai holes in it I gave up trying to reshape the branches!

We played games such as speak out! The kids all went up to Scott's man cave and played pool, but Kai of course had to keep to his routine and wanted his bath. We were all so thankful that he was here with us, as I don't think any of us thought we would be as lucky as we were.

After being told so many times to say goodbye to Kai here he was, a face full of chocolate, hiccupping loads as he was so full, splashing around in a bath full of bubbles and smiling in contentment. I would never take any day for granted again.

2017

With a new year came a new us. We were determined this was going to be our year. After the horror of the year before I couldn't wait to make new memories! It started off great! My lovely Facebook friend Teri had nominated Kai for a 'be brave bear' through a charity.

Kai had been accepted and was sent a lovely blue dinosaur with all the words associated to him across its tummy. Loved, beautiful, star, fearless, precious gift, cherished, courageous, special and brave. St Begh's Junior School in Whitehaven had brought it for Kai through the charity.

I was so blown away by Teri's nomination, and for the school for being so kind and buying a gift for someone they knew nothing about! I sent them a thank you email with a picture of Kai next to his bear smiling that cheeky smile of his.

Kai's birthday was coming up and I couldn't quite believe he was going to now be fifteen, today was an equally special day as Kai shares his birthday with Jude, Beckie's son.

I never thought Kai would see this birthday, after the previous year in Great Ormond Street, and he was made a huge fuss of. We ordered a huge chocolate cake from The Cakey Lady who, as usual, went all out and made it that extra special. It had all Kai's favourite chocolate treats on, such as Bueno, KitKat, chocolate buttons and Flakes. It was topped with a crown on, a big colourful number fifteen and 'King Kai'. We all gathered at the table, video recorder and camera ready to capture another special milestone.

Kai's face when the cake was brought out with lots of candles on was priceless. We placed it in front of him singing 'Happy birthday' at the top of our voices. He looked at the cake in shock and before any of us could react he grabbed a handful of chocolate fingers and stuffed them straight into his mouth as fast as he could. We were crying with laughter and the kids were all clapping while Kai sat beaming with a face full of chocolate.

Beckie had arranged a big party for Jude with a magician so we all went to that while Scott went off to work. Kai looked so smart in his vintage car shirt, green chinos and his hair neatly gelled. Every time I looked at him I felt such pride that I had made such a gorgeous child.

The children had so much fun joining in and playing games, while Kai was being fed sneakily, and early, from the buffet. Whenever Kai went to a party he would look around with his big eyes for a soft touch to take the bait and come and sit and feed him, it worked every time!

Kai then had a huge seizure in his wheelchair, it was so violent and aggressive, his body shook and he looked petrified. During a seizure he would now completely wet through his nappy. Even if his nappy was dry he would flood through it and he would be covered from neck to toe in urine. He would also sleep for a long time as the seizure was so aggressive.

Beckie and her mum, Dot, helped me lift Kai behind a curtain where we cleaned him up, changed him and tilted him in his chair so he could sleep it off.

While everyone was still running around having fun and eating, Kai slept through. Beckie made him up a huge plate of food to take home so he wouldn't miss out on his favourite part of a party.

I was so angry that his seizures were now so unrelenting, any time, any day, including birthdays, Kai would have now very frightening seizures. I was used to seeing him have seizures from four months of age, but even for me the latest ones were scary.

They were uncontrollable and exhausting for him. He would drop and slam to the floor, shaking and banging his head repeatedly while I tried to protect him from further injury. Many times, he had a bumped head, black eyes, bruised back and split lips.

Even with his amazing helmet (my friend, Rachel, got him through a go fund me page) which protected his head so much, he couldn't wear it all the time. Sometimes, it felt like the seizure knew this and would wait for that very minute I took it off to bath him or change his nappy.

Kai was so tall now, which he just loved to show off about it. This made it harder as when he had a seizure he was falling from a greater height. Kai was now 5ft 5", the same height as Scott and I, but as he walked on tip toes he seemed a lot taller.

He found this hilarious and would come over and size us both up, he would stand right up to you on tip toes, raise his chin and laugh. We would then have to make a huge fuss about how tall he was, he would laugh and give you a smug smile. If he was sitting down and you went to cuddle him, again he would give you a smug smile and raise his chin to show you how small you were in comparison to him!

My brother, Harry, and my sister, Lily-Rose, were towering above Kai but he would still insist he was the tallest. Sometimes, Harry would prove him wrong and stand his 6' 4" self over Kai, he would look at him in disgust and walk away! With Lily-Rose he would grab her in a head lock hug and then lift his chin above her as if to say, see I told you I was the tallest!

Sometimes I would be minding my own business and Kai would come up to me and lift his chin up, then smile down on me and run off laughing. He loved a swear word, he would cry laughing if you called him a little sod or a little shit.

So, I would call him a little shit and he would hold his belly crying with laughter. Beckie, Scott and I would often playfully shout an insult at him when he was naughty, and he would cry real tears of laughter and joy.

We used to say imagine if anyone heard how we talked to him, they would think we were horrid to him! If we were out and Kai was being his cheeky self, I would whisper a naughty word into his ear and that would set him off holding his belly, both of us laughing at our secret joke.

Kai's bowels were still a worry, even though he was going to the toilet regularly I was concerned. He had started to bring his food back up after eating which set alarm bells off. He was still on sachets of Movicol, yet we still had no regular appointments or check-ups, and no community nurses coming in.

I hadn't been taught to check his tummy properly, which even if I had I still wouldn't have been happy, as so many times his tummy was checked and yet a two-litre blockage was inside him! One day as I was showering Kai I noticed his tummy looked very swollen. Instantly, dread washed over me in waves.

He was skinny everywhere else, still putting on weight at a steady pace, but looking at him now his tummy was swollen and protruding I called Scott into the shower room to look at him. I was known to over react when it came to Kai and over-analyse every little thing. Scott agreed his tummy was swollen, I instantly got him out of the shower, dried him and lay him on the floor.

Pressing his tummy, he happily lay chewing the towel while my heart hammered so fast in my chest I thought it would shoot out at any moment. I could feel a hard mass in his tummy for sure, I felt sick and confused. He was still opening his bowels why, and how, had this happened? Not every day but that didn't concern me, not everyone has a bowel movement every day, and he was filling his nappy enough for me to not be worried.

Now I was questioning myself, did he do enough at every nappy change? Did it just look like a lot but if done in the toilet you could see it wasn't? I took pictures of him laying down, standing up, on his side and sent them straight to Beckie. She instantly replied that yes, he did look swollen but maybe he was blocked from today? I dried and dressed him, the little monkey was loving all the attention and thinking mummy was tickling him.

I decided to give him a couple of days and see how he was, I didn't want to rush in and look silly when he was opening his bowels and it certainly didn't look or smell like over flow as it had before. I sent Kai to school as usual and phoned them explaining my concerns. They kept a close eye on him and agreed he looked swollen.

The next day I kept him off school and all morning he was sick. I knew straight away that this was not a good sign at all. I took him straight to the hospital, I wasn't taking any chances. Last time there had been no signs at all that Kai's bowel were blocked, he was happy, he was still eating, drinking and in no sign of distress at all. This time there were signs and to me that was a blessing.

As soon as I got to the hospital and explained why we were there I knew it wasn't seen as urgent. I couldn't understand how it couldn't be when only a year ago to the very week we were being blue lighted to Great Ormond Street Hospital while Kai's organs struggled to stay working.

After being observed they weren't concerned enough to keep Kai in, I was exhausted and battered with the constant fighting and being over-looked. I was told they were at full capacity, to take Kai home and they would call me with a plan.

I didn't like it one bit but had no other choice and did what they said. I had been at the hospital all day fighting Kai's corner, and even given them a copy of his notes to say how dangerous and quick his last hospital stay was. No obvious symptoms yet Kai was on life support as quick as that, now he was actually showing symptoms and my gut was screaming at me to do something, anything not to take him home.

I had no choice so home we went. I kept Kai at home for two days constantly phoning our two local hospitals to try and see if he could be admitted, I was told that they were both full. If I was to take him to the hospital further away he wouldn't be seen, as they too were full. At this point I was so upset and frustrated and I told my good friend, Paula, how I was feeling. Straight away she typed an email for me to send to the hospitals PALS department, which I did.

To whom this may concern,

My son, Kai Hammond, has a bowel impaction. He currently has a distended stomach, is struggling to pass stools and is lethargic. He has complex disabilities and a history of a rupture of the bowel, leading to life threatening sepsis and a lengthy stay in PICU and GOSH.

I am flabbergasted with this history we are now being left to cope alone with no back up. This isn't because he is safe at home, this is because our local hospitals don't have any beds for a child at such high risk.

What stuns me even more is the attitude of passing the buck and it not being anyone problem. It is my problem and Kai is at high risk of recurrence of life-threatening complications.

Please take urgent action before he becomes seriously ill. I am desperate for him to receive timely, and caring, medical attention, not to be used as a pawn between two hospitals, which seem to forget he is a person with the right to appropriate medical care. I look forward to a resolution between the hospitals by 3pm today.

Are you waiting for him to become so ill his life will be at risk again? I am sure that will make for an interesting court case for negligence in the future. I am a desperate mum of a complex child who is deteriorating, please someone take responsibility and move this on.

Vikki Hammond

Paula had always been great at the bureaucracy of hospitals and I always turned to her for help and guidance, which even today she is there for me.

The following day Kai was still throwing up, I was changing his tops constantly and now his nappy was also dry. His seizures had got to the point where he would be dry all day and then have a huge one that would flood through his nappy. I was told this was common with people with disabilities to hold in their urine, now I was worrying he had a blockage and it was preventing him from emptying his bladder. I phoned the hospital again, they were supposed to call me. I was told to keep him at home and they would call me once they had a plan in place. It wasn't good enough and I marched him straight back to the hospital.

At this point, I think the hospital were fed up of seeing me and picking up my calls, they put me in a side room. I was told not to feed Kai or let him have anything to drink. We sat for hours, with them only bothering to check in on us once. I was now at boiling point and dangerously close to losing my shit, which takes a lot for me to do.

I hate upsetting people, complaining and making a nuisance of myself, but my mind was racing as all I could picture was Kai on life support, tubes covering every inch of his beautiful face. There was no way I was having that happen to him again.

By this point I had been at the hospital for hours and I completely lost it. I pulled a junior in and demanded to know why the hell I wasn't being listened to - how serious did it have to get before they would act? Why were we placed into a side room and left all bloody day, with a child that had no idea why he couldn't drink or eat a thing? We both hadn't eaten or drank for seven hours at this point and I was livid.

The response I got made me shake with anger; they had forgotten about us. The entire day we were sat there with not even a nurse coming in to see us and we were forgotten! My face turned red, my heart hammered in my chest and my head was pounding. I'd had enough of this shit, it wasn't bloody good enough, yes, I understood they were busy. I know how under-staffed they can be, the waiting room was jam packed with people waiting to be seen, but this was urgent!

This wasn't a sprained ankle or a sore throat this was life or death and every minute counted. At this point they realised I wouldn't be going home, not of my own accord anyway. I wasn't leaving until Kai had been X-rayed and fully checked, I wasn't taking no for an answer and I wasn't being fobbed off with them just feeling his tummy as that isn't an indication of what was going on inside.

The junior went to get a Doctor, who I could tell was pissed off at this angry woman who wouldn't just take their word for it. I told them I wasn't going home, I went home the day before and his symptoms had worsened, I had spent the entire night in his bed in case he was sick in his sleep. I had spent the morning waiting for a phone call that never came, and quite frankly wouldn't come as I knew full well they didn't have a bloody plan in place.

Busy or not, tough we were there now, and I wasn't leaving until Kai was X-rayed. My pleas fell on deaf ears, although feeling for themselves they could feel his bowels were impacted yet they wouldn't X-ray him. I told them to phone Kai's bowel team in GOSH and come up with a plan with them, as I was staying put.

At this point Scott phoned me after sorting the kids out with my wonderful step-mum, Terri. When I explained to him what had happened he was livid and said he would be with us as soon as he could. I knew once Scott got to the hospital and had seen how we weren't being listened to he would completely lose his shit as well.

I was constantly updating Beckie by text and phone, she too was disgusted. The Doctor agreed to transfer me into the children's ward and keep Kai overnight while she phoned GOSH to see what they could do from there. Thank goodness we were, at last, one foot in the door and wouldn't be sent home and ignored.

The children's ward was amazing, and I could not fault them at all, straight away a nurse came over and apologised for everything. Obviously, it wasn't their fault and now I had calmed down I knew the hospital was very busy, but all I wanted was for Kai to be checked over.

It was now evening time and Kai was placed on the ward. He had to sit and watch children eating and drinking, and I felt such guilt. He didn't understand why he couldn't have anything, and right now neither did I. No plan was in place, I had starved him all day for nothing and I mentioned it to the nurses.

By now, my beautiful friend who works at the hospital, and I won't name, had been in contact with the ward and explained everything. I had been keeping her updated all day, as well, and bless her I will never forget what she done for us, as the nurses who were already so lovely to us went all out.

They moved us onto a closed ward and opened it just for us, they could see Kai was fed up of being stuck in his wheelchair all day. He had free run of the entire ward and had sandwiches, crisps, chocolate and drink brought out for him. He ate everything they had on offer and was happily skipping around the ward.

24

He walked straight over to the nurse who was sat with us, looked into her eyes and said, "Yeah baby," in his Jamaican accent. This had us all in stitches and I think she fell a little bit in love with him. Kai would say 'Lola' and 'Yeah baby,' in his accent, we called it his Patrick Truman voice (from Eastenders) as they sounded so alike!

We were soon talk of the ward with the nurses and one after the other they came in to apologise, to make us comfortable and ask for details to get things moving. They did more for us in one hour than A&E had done in two days.

They explained they were on the phone to GOSH as we spoke and that the current plan was to admit Kai for the night and give him an enema to see if that would shift the blockage. The Doctor would be down to see us soon, and instantly I felt like a huge weight had been lifted from my shoulders, finally someone was listening to us!

The nurse came back into the ward and was furious, she said the Doctor who was supposed to be dealing with Kai had now gone home for the day. She was so angry she was nearly in tears, which by now I very nearly was to! She was disgusted we had been left and forgotten about, especially after talking to Great Ormond Street Hospital and hearing how serious this situation was.

She had told one of the other nurses to call the Doctor at home and explain herself. She also told me that the bowel team from GOSH were taking no chances whatsoever and were to send Kai for an urgent X-ray. I cried tears of happiness, that's all I wanted in the first place, just to know the size of the blockage and then come up with a plan of action.

I also told her that we had no social worker, no community nurses, no local support and no one to call if we had any concerns. She was outraged and straight away put in an assessment for community nurses, social worker, a local paediatrician and bowel team.

All I wanted was someone to listen to me and now they finally were, Kai went down for his X-ray completely oblivious to all the commotion fuss and worry. He loved X-rays as he got to lay down and relax in a dimly lit room.

Afterwards, we were taken back to the ward where Kai continued to make use of the completely empty space. Flapping his hands and running in circles, I sometimes looked at him and was so glad he would never feel pain, worry or loss. He would never have his heart broken, would never worry about money or bills or work. I would never have to share him.

Scott and I had plans for once the three of us were older. We would buy a camper van and drive around the UK taking in the scenes, eating chips on the beach with the sand between our toes. Just the three of us together. We couldn't take Kai abroad as it was too much of a risk and a worry. If something happened while we were overseas, I couldn't even imagine what we would do.

The nurse broke my thoughts and snapped me back to reality when she said the results were back. She took me over to her computer screen and pulled up Kai's X-ray and straight away I knew this wasn't good news. Kai had another blockage right up to his chest, I felt sick, my head started to spin, and I leant on the counter to balance myself.

I felt so much guilt, how had this happened again? How had I not seen the signs before? The nurse was talking to me, but I couldn't hear her, I could see the tears in her eyes and feel the touch of her hand on my arm, but my head was spinning. I managed to compose myself enough to ask, "How?" How could this possibly have happened? Why was this allowed to happen? Where was our follow up care plan, and all the things we were promised when Kai had come off life support?

Things started to move quickly now, and it was decided we would be admitted onto the ward, which for one gave me great concern as Kai couldn't sleep safely in a normal bed. He would stand up and once while in hospital two days after major brain surgery he stood up and fell straight off the bed and smashed his head. Ever since then I had asked for a room, with a low bed or a mattress on the floor which we would share.

For health and safety this wasn't possible as all the rooms were full. This is one thing I find very hard to understand. If a child or adult has complex medical needs and requires a setting as safe as possible this cannot be made possible in a hospital.

I understand that hospitals are very busy places, and the cost of such equipment is high, but for those out there that couldn't sleep in a normal single bed it is a huge deal. The nurses were amazing and trying their best to accommodate Kai's needs as another nurse phoned GOSH to update them of his results. I rang Scott, Terri and Beckie and updated them on the latest news. No-one could quite believe this had happened again, almost a year to the very day.

The nurse came back from her phone call and told me there was a change of plan. Kai was now going to be blue lighted to Great Ormond Street hospital as the bowel team there explained how serious this could be. They wanted to give Kai the enemas and observe him for a couple of nights.

Now I had to phone Scott and ask for an overnight bag for the both of us. We were both livid that Kai, again, had been failed. I was in so much of a rage that at that point it time I could quite easily have gone on a rampage!

Scott came with my brother, Harry, and Kai was over the moon to see them both, he ran straight up to Scott and took him by the hand to the nearest door. Scott told him, "No, I can't take you home," and Kai was ignoring him and leading him to every door he could see. It was if he was saying "I've bloody well had enough of this place now"!

When that wasn't working, he walked over to Harry who was still over six feet tall. He stood on his tip toes and tried to show Harry how tall he was - it failed! He didn't even reach Harry's nose, he gave Harry a filthy look and walked off in disgust. We were laughing at Kai's facial expressions, for a child with very limited one worded speech the boy could say a thousand words with his face.

THE FIGHT

We were transferred from our local hospital to GOSH, I had hugged Scott tight and felt sick that, yet again, the children would wake to no mummy at home. I always felt torn in two, I would never leave Kai's side for a minute in hospital as no one knew Kai like I did. He would also drive everyone mad and get up to all sorts if I did leave him, all night parties and slapping nurse's bums.

I was also fully aware that leaving the kids with no notice was having a huge effect on them all. Daisy and Honey-Mae took it the hardest and had become very clingy; I had to hide the fact that I had a hospital appointment as Daisy would get herself in a state and be convinced I would be gone again for weeks or months on end.

I had missed so many firsts with the kids that I often felt, and do still feel, guilty for. I missed Honey-Mae's first day at school, school plays and discos. So much that I would never get back, as if they fell on a hospital appointment stay or day I had to always put Kai first. I often wonder if they feel resentment for that, or self-doubt that I loved him more. I like to think they don't, I like to think they will, and do, know I always tried my best for them, but if they did resent me I couldn't blame them.

The children's ward at our local hospital had been amazing and I couldn't fault them, there were tears and hugs as we left them to head to GOSH.

As we pulled up outside GOSH in the ambulance I felt sick to my stomach that a year ago to the very day we were back here. I was alone and scared again. Scott had to be at home to give the kids a routine, and my step-mum, Terri, was there by his side helping with the children.

Scott of course has always come to be with us during the day, but we both agreed this time one of us needed to be there for when the kids finish school. Beckie as usual, was amazing and constantly checking in to see if anything was needed, and to listen to me rage down the phone to her.

We were given a small room, which I instantly felt relieved about, at least Kai wouldn't keep anyone awake and I could concentrate on him rather than upsetting anyone else! Nurses were in and out all night and the bowel team came in to administer an enema. They were going to do this throughout the night and see how he got on with clearing out the blockage.

I was so angry with them for the lack of follow up care but too tired at this point to bring it up, it would wait until the morning. I hardly slept as every time I got into bed, I would hear Kai grunting and lots of wind! I must have changed him and the bed with the nurses help around six times. We were both covered in shit! I was relieved it was having an effect at least. We both managed about half an hour sleep and then Kai was up at 5am bright and early shouting, "Lola!"

Although Kai was given 2-3 enemas throughout the night which had little effect, I was devastated. Even though he had cleared a good amount out of himself his X-ray was still showing enough faeces in him to concern them.

We had options and I wanted to go with the less invasive and upsetting for Kai, he had already been through too much. It was decided that Kai would be put to sleep and taken down to theatre where a manual evacuation would be performed. The bowel team thought that giving Kai an operation was very high risk, which Scott and I both agreed.

This would mean a finger, or more would be inserted into Kai and his bowels would be gently emptied. If all was well, we would then be allowed home the following day. I took this as my opportunity to tell them how unhappy I was at being left alone with no support in place for a child with complex needs and now the added worry of his bowel issues. I wanted a plan in place before I left the hospital, an appointment made, community nurses and a bloody social worker for Christ's sake! I was told that a plan would be put in place and we would discuss it later that day when Kai was out of theatre.

Watching Kai be wheeled off to theatre never ever got any easier over the years, I could never get used to it. Scott was always the one to take him into a room to be put to sleep and to kiss his head. I couldn't cope with it, he looked so vulnerable and so trusting, smiling away flapping his hands not a clue at what was about to happen to him. At least this time Kai would be out in an hour and pain free, just a little groggy.

We both sat on the ward in the room waiting for the phone to ring to say he was out of theatre. Both of us still very angry and upset that we had been failed so badly. I don't blame anyone in particular, or even a certain hospital. I am grateful for all they had done over the years for Kai, it just always seemed to be him that slipped through the net and was forgotten about. I received a message from PALS department about my email of complaint, the lady wrote that they would be looking into my concerns and getting back to us. To this very day I am still waiting...

Kai was out of theatre and wide-awake complaining that he didn't have chips on his arrival. Looking around I could tell what his eyes were wandering around the room for!

The bowel team came in to talk to Scott and I and we were very honest with them. They agreed that Kai had slipped through the net and that a plan needed to be put in place.

We were told that Kai needed an enema for the next couple of weeks, to be done at home by me which they would train me for. I stopped him right there, there was no way on this earth I was administering an enema to Kai, he had not long had a bowel operation! I wasn't having the responsibility of getting it wrong, I wanted someone to make sure it was done correctly and to check his tummy while he had it done. I needed to know that Kai was now going to the toilet enough and wasn't impacted again.

Dr Greg could see I wasn't backing down and said that he would put referrals in for a community nurse to administer it at home, or his school nurse could do it at school. I was also told that Kai would need to be on six sachets of Movicola day, and lactulose 3 times a day. Also, they wanted me to seriously consider Kai for an A.C.E. tube.

I was told that an A.C.E. tube was an operation which would create a channel (usually using the appendix) into the large bowel. A fluid is then used to flush out the bowel and could be inserted into the A.C.E. This would mean a couple of hours a day on the toilet flushing out Kai's bowel. It also meant another operation and another scar to add to his body, I was devastated but willing to do anything possible to prevent this from happening again. We were discharged the following day, and I felt so much more positive that with the right help and local support another blockage could be avoided.

Back home the following day Kai had a huge seizure and continuously banged his head on the floor, his seizures were now becoming uncontrollable and I really didn't like the aggressiveness of his latest ones. I protected his head as much as I could, but with all the thrashing and banging he ended up with a black eye and a spilt lip.

I felt like once I had started to deal with one problem more would arise. At that moment in time my priority was his bowel, as I knew how quickly he could deteriorate. I felt terrible sending him back to school the state he was in, luckily the school were so understanding and supportive as usual.

They were also relieved Kai's blockage had been removed as like me, they were also terrified. My mental health at this point was through the roof, although on the outside people couldn't tell as I always plastered on a smile. Inside I was panicky, anxious and living on edge. I felt like I had a huge responsibility and Kai's life was literally in my hands. I had to make sure he went to the toilet, that he went enough, and make sure he had the correct dosage of medication at the correct times.

The Movicol Kai hated, and now it was upped to six sachets a day I was fighting a losing battle, I did everything advised to me, and even went online for advice. He knew they were mixed in food, or drink and would instantly spit them straight out. I was advised online to try chocolate Movicol, I mixed this with Kai's milkshakes I gave him to help him gain weight and thank goodness he didn't guess and gulped the lot! I also added double cream and full fat milk to his milkshake and upped his shakes to three a day, his plates were fully loaded, and I sent him into school with fat food!

It started to work, soon his weight was not far off eight stone, his cheeks filled out and he looked so much healthier. Although as he'd had a growth spurt and was now 5ft 5" he could really have done with another stone on him! I used to call him Bambi legs as his legs would bend inwards and he was so tall and slim, or giraffe legs. Usually mixed in with a swear word, and Kai would laugh and laugh.

Kai's bed was now an issue, although his safe space had been a life saver to us, I now found it a burden. I was worried as I couldn't have a video monitor set up as the steel frame interrupted the signal on the aerial. Kai was also now so big and tall it was almost impossible for me to lift him out of his bed. The mattress was at floor level, and he used this to his advantage, I would go into wake him up and he would roll over and look as if to say, "Do your best!"

I was physically struggling so bad. Scott's back was still not great, and I took the decision to do Kai's care alone, as I couldn't risk Scott being off work because we couldn't afford it. I tried the occupational therapists, but the bed would cost around £10,000 and there was a lot of red tape to go through.

Some days Kai would have a seizure and I would literally have to carry a boy the same height as me on my own. He would sleep through the whole wash and dress routine and it would take me hours to get him ready. I was struggling physically as well as mentally. I loved this boy with all my heart and I knew I would never ever have him apart from me, but I knew that now more than ever I needed equipment and outside help.

Beckie had always been amazing and direct payments had funded for her to come in a couple of times a week to help with Kai. It was time for that to end, Beckie's hours at work had increased and she had a full-on job role. I needed someone to come in the mornings not after school, as the mornings were the hardest. I would be up at 6.00am to get four kids ready and sit down with a sigh of relief that we had made the school rush, only for Kai to have a huge seizure and wet through all his clothes. I would then have to start the process all over again of washing him, his clothes, his chair, the floor and whatever else his urine had soaked.

Some days I was physically done in; I pulled my shoulder, my knee, and my back was also not great. I knew that a new bed for Kai would completely change our lives. I could get him up easily and not have to lift half as much. I also knew now that I needed hoists and some other equipment to help.

We both had a few tears as Beckie had been there through everything since Kai was two years old, silly really as we still saw her every single week, but it was an end of an era for us! Kai didn't care, Beckie would still pop over on a Saturday and he would walk straight to the bathroom and shout until she gave in and ran him a bath. For him nothing had changed, Beckie was still his bitch!

My beautiful friend Hailey, who I had only ever met once at my friend Jodie's mum's EastEnders-themed party, saw my post on Facebook about my struggles. I always felt better after a rant as usually someone would come up with a great idea or solution to my problem. She phoned me up and mentioned that a charity her sister had worked for was now closing and was there anything we needed to help us with Kai. Obviously, a bed was out of the question as they were so expensive. I couldn't think of a thing as we needed equipment that costs thousands of pounds to make our life's easier.

She wouldn't give up and by the end of the phone call and listening to all the problems we faced with lack of help we came up with the idea of a safer outside area for Kai. His room backed into the garden, and he has patio doors that opened out onto the decking. The trouble was the decking had no rails or slopes for Kai's bad days when he needed to be in his wheelchair. He also didn't like sitting out there as the sun was too much for him. By the end of the call Hailey had it all pictured in her head what he needed. I remember hanging the phone up thinking what an amazing thing to have done for someone that she hardly knew. I wouldn't yet understand what an amazing friend I had gained through that call.

The following day Hailey phoned back. She had gone to bed thinking about our struggles and it had played on her mind. She was shocked to hear that we had no support in place or equipment to help us and she felt she had to help. She had spent the night looking up specially made beds for children with special needs. She found an amazing charity called Newlife that loaned out beds for six months and then helped you to find a grant to have your own new one! I couldn't believe it, it was that easy!

As I got to know Hailey I realised that once she has an idea in her head that's it, it's happening no matter what! She phoned the charity of her own accord and got them to call me, and just like that a ten-minute phone call had us a bed on loan for six months. I couldn't believe it! This was going to change our whole lives!

We decided on a full-sized single bed, like a hospital bed, one that could move up and down with a remote control. We would be able to use a video monitor with this bed. It was also adapted for us, the sides literally came up to the ceiling, so Kai couldn't climb out, it was also fully padded inside so if Kai had any accidents I could spray and wipe it clean. The thought of having a video monitor excited me more than anything, no more worrying, sleeping with him or checking him. I would now be able to see him and hear him fully from any room in the house!

It was a battle to get the occupational therapists to sign a form to say Kai needed this bed, as again it was all red tape. After weeks of phone calls, we finally managed to get a signature, the bed was ordered and would be delivered in a weeks' time! I couldn't believe our luck, this was going to be the start of us getting more help and much needed equipment, I was sure of it.

My anxiety was now coming back at night and I would wake up in a blind panic. My heart would beat so fast and then slow right down until I was convinced it would stop altogether. I was a walking wreck, I also had the feeling that I would find Kai dead in his bed. I was terrified and every morning when I got up if I couldn't hear him I would get myself into a state.

My PTSD was at an all-time high and I broke down to Beckie over the phone, I told her my fears of Kai dying and she reassured me and made me speak to Scott. I knew she was right, as I was snappy and irritable in the mornings, taking my fears out on Scott when he had no idea why. Once I told him I instantly felt better, he reassured me and got up with me each morning for the next couple of months. Him going in first to check on Kai and then me getting him out of bed and carrying on with our day.

I couldn't shake the feeling and, in the end, went straight to my GP who rushed me through to receive counselling. I knew that with Kai being on life support that time it had played havoc with me mentally the last couple of years.

He prescribed me some beta blockers which really helped to calm me down. Now all I needed to do was to say the words out loud to someone that wouldn't judge me, who would listen, and my words wouldn't affect them in any way. I felt so lucky to have such amazing friends and family that supported me in so many ways. I often felt like such a burden, everyone was expecting me to be happy Kai was still alive, and I felt angry with myself for not living each day to the fullest, especially when Kai would get up with a big smile on his face. Why couldn't I just be happy he was still here? Why did my mind constantly go back to him on life support? I was so aware now that everything I had taken for granted before could change in an instant and I couldn't shake the feeling off that something bad would happen to my boy. Counselling couldn't come soon enough for me.

The day of the bed arrival came, we were so excited! I knew how much Kai's safe space cost, which was well over £10,000, and still selling for quite a bit of money. Although the money would have come in handy I was also aware that this could benefit another family that was struggling like we were. So, I donated it to the occupational therapists who already had a family lined up to have it. It made me happy that the safe space that had helped us so very much over the years would now be going to another family which in turn would also change their lives. We cleared the room out ready for the arrival, I had splashed out on black and white print Danger Mouse bed covers and new sheets. I also sent Hailey a big bunch of flowers which, after all he had done for us, didn't seem enough! We had also chosen a lovely man called Brendan from ATG to design and make Kai his very own decking area thanks to Hailey and her sister, who kindly thought of Kai.

Kai's bed arrived and once it was up I cried tears of joy, as did Scott. It was perfect; and they had also added wheels, so we could wheel it away from the wall and clean under it. We spent the afternoon putting Kai's bedroom back together and making his bed. It looked just like a castle which was perfect for our lazy boy who we called King Kai. It was light wood with the softest suede in light beige all inside, I knew Kai would love running his hands over that and taking in the feel of the material. The fact that I could now raise the bed would mean Kai would be at my waist length or higher if I wanted and I could swivel his legs around and get him straight out of bed. No more laughing at me and ignoring me when I called his name and pleaded with him every morning to "get up for school, little monkey". We placed Kai's video monitor in the corner of his bed and spent the next hour positioning it, so I could see Kai from all angles. We made sure we could hear from the other rooms and we discovered that it had a control, so you could change the angle and scan his room. I could then have the mini tv with me and watch him all evening and check on him into the night, which was so much better for all of us.

Kai came home, and straight away Scott took him into his bedroom to show him his new bed. He walked past it, glanced at it and walked out in disgust. We captured it all on video - all you can hear is me in the background laughing at his reaction. We then put Kai into his bed and showed him that the bed could be raised and lowered, and how much easier it would be for me to get him up in the mornings. At this Kai looked at us in shock and I could see it sinking in his little mind that now, he would be up and dressed without me bribing him or lifting him up! He hopped off the bed and walked off shouting "Mum" in an angry voice - he really wasn't impressed at all! That first night I felt so much better than I had done in months, I checked on him throughout the night and could hear him singing to himself when he woke up in the morning. Words cannot describe how much that bed and the kind gesture Hailey and Newlife did for us.

My counselling started which was a huge help to me, and I enjoyed having an hour to myself every week to get all the poison out of my mind that had been festering. I was full of rage as we still had no local support despite all the promises that were made to us. The school nurses weren't keen to do Kai's enema at school and I agreed, as he would then have an hour of travelling home in a dirty nappy. Community nurses told me they didn't come out for bowel issues and I rightly or wrongly lost my shit. I put tweets on twitter and with Paula's help I tagged to allow the appropriate people to see my tweets and shared our fight. I tweeted that we had no local support in place, no equipment and no social worker. Soon I had phone calls which I took as no coincidence, the bowel team now wanted to see us the following week for a check-up that should have already been made! The occupational therapist phoned and offered us changing tables and referred us to our local council to have hoists put in. We were also offered mobile hoists for now, and a lovely lady on Facebook dropped off a shower chair for Kai to use until the OT had them back in stock. The community nurses, after much fighting, also agreed to come out and visit Kai to see what we needed. As for social services, I rang them up in tears begging them for some help; I couldn't fight all these people for what Kai desperately needed for him to be safe and cared for at home.

Scott still couldn't help as his back was so bad, and I know he felt immense guilt that he couldn't help me, but my priority was Scott staying in work. I screamed at them that for me to hand Kai over to them would cost them over £350,000 a year! All I was asking for was some help a couple of times a week in the mornings when Kai's seizures were at their worst; some support and some back up regarding equipment too! Kai was now 15 and not going to get any smaller. I poured my heart out during that phone call sobbing and pleading for any kind of help they could offer, because at that moment we had nothing and none. It did the trick and I was given a social worker, and a meeting was arranged through the school which all Kai's consultants, social worker, occupational therapist teams could attend.

That was all I wanted; why did I have to scream and shout to get any support at all? Scott was helping as best he could, but his back was so bad, and I know he felt immense guilt for that, but my priority was for Scott to work and earn money.

Kai's meeting was held at the school and I took Adele with me for support. Kai's teacher attended as well as the newly appointed social worker and an occupational therapist. I was devastated his consultants couldn't attend and felt like the whole morning was a waste of time. His teacher did an amazing job of telling the social worker that they themselves struggled with Kai with equipment, and she didn't understand how I was doing it all alone at home with nothing. The OT was very supportive, and I have never blamed them. There are so many boxes that need ticking and criteria to be met that any family really don't stand a chance of a hint of help. We talked about Kai's seizures and how much stronger they now were. Once he'd had one he now slept a lot longer. It was harder to move him and change him after he had flooded through his clothes. We also talked about Kai's bowel and how I had decided against having an ACE tube fitted. The school nurse agreed. To try and get Kai to sit for a long period of time on the toilet would not be possible, especially once he'd had a nasty seizure. If Kai were to have any operation it would have to be something like a colostomy bag which I could change along with his nappy, and that wouldn't be hindered by him being asleep during the change. I came away deflated, and Adele was gobsmacked by the lack of people attending the meeting and all the talk of criteria's, etc. As an outsider looking in it must have seemed crazy, but for someone that was used to being told no and living the life, it was just another fight on our hands to us.

The community nurses came out to visit us and after a long talk agreed that Kai would have enemas as and when he needed them. The bowel team had been in touch with me and knew I was against the ACE tube, and after hearing my reasons agreed that we would review Kai carefully with the community nurses full support and then go from there. I knew that with a close eye on Kai he would be fine with his bowels, and he was also put under the care of a local bowel team at Addenbrookes hospital that would review him every few months as well as GOSH. Kai's new plan was now six sachets of Movicol, lactulose and suppositories to be given by me a few times a week. If Kai was still having trouble opening his bowels I could ring the community nurses who would come out and give him an enema. That is all I wanted, I felt beaten down and tired that it had taken all my energy to get basic little things put in place for Kai to avoid the same situation from reoccurring again.

I then got a letter from Social services a few weeks later; we were no longer having a social worker. I didn't even have the energy to argue any more, they felt that we weren't a family in need and signed us off to the short breaks team. This was all pointless to me as Kai didn't have respite. It makes me so sad that in this day and age there are so many families out there with no support in place for them at all, and if you do ask for help you are seen as a nuisance. It took every ounce of me to say after fifteen years of struggling, "I am not ok," and now we were back where we started, alone. We were now on the local councils list for hoists and I was told there would be around a three year wait for us. By now I had given up and just shrugged my shoulders in defeat.

The occupational therapists were amazing, and I really did feel for them, they had tried their hardest to get us pushed up the list, but their hands were tied. We were number sixty-two, and with an already delayed start to the year we were by no means going to be getting hoists anytime soon. We tried a mobile hoist for now but that wasn't suitable - Kai was too heavy to wheel in it and it got stuck on the carpet. We were also given a bigger and safer shower chair which was an amazing help for when Kai had a seizure and was too tired to stand up. They also thought that with the hoists we should knock down the bathroom wall and have them running from Kai's room straight into the shower room and a changing table could then be used, which would ease my back a little as bending on the floor really wasn't doing it any favours! Again, I couldn't get my hopes up as this was going to be in a few years' time. For now, we would just have to struggle on.

SUNSHINE AFTER THE RAIN

After the trials of the last few months we decided to take the children on two holidays during the coming year. One of the holidays would be to Butlins in Bognor Regis. I had fond memories of this place as my Nan took me when I was ten and I hadn't been back since. We asked the school if we could take them out for a week in June, something I had never done before. I wanted it to be quieter as Kai and Bailey weren't great with crowds and lots of noise. This was Bailey's final few weeks in primary school and the school had been amazing helping me with his EHCP, which was a very lengthy and long process. I was worried about sending Bailey to mainstream secondary school as I know how cruel kids can be, and with his autism and Tourette's final few weeks left in primary school and the school had been amazing helping me with his EHCP, a very lengthy and long process. I was worried about sending Bailey to main stream secondary school as I know how cruel kids can be, and with his autism and Tourette's I knew he would stick out. I also was worried about sending him to our local special-needs school, as there was nothing suitable for him locally. The problem was he was three years behind in school work, so he didn't really need a special-needs school, but he wasn't far ahead to cope well in mainstream education. It seemed to me it was either a school more for behavioural problems or mainstream. How I wished there was a school similar to Kai's who were amazing, and I couldn't fault. I had spent the last few months visiting schools and although I worried myself silly I applied for a local mainstream school. I didn't want to put him somewhere he would be out of his depth, I had visited the local special needs school and didn't get as far as the waiting room. A child was swearing and being carried out by a group of teachers after punching a student and attacking a teacher. I watched the scene unfold in front of me and pictured Bailey in the middle of it all, so I got up and ran back to the van. I hadn't even had a chance to take off my visitor's badge! In hindsight I should have followed through with the visit, but it scared me to think of my child in a school which so clearly catered for behavioural issues, something Bailey didn't have. A holiday was very much needed!

Butlins was just as I remembered, right on the sea front with so much to do! We were very fortunate that we had booked the week that there was a heatwave. We had a ground floor chalet and a shower which was great, as lifting Kai in and out of the bath alone was becoming very difficult. Scott had sciatica and would have bouts of pain, I had never seen him cry tears of pain before and seeing a grown man crawling around on the floor was horrendous. I didn't want to risk his back, so I was sorting out Kai all alone, which now he was so tall was becoming a lot harder.

A few weeks before our holiday Kai had finally got the wheelchair I had been desperate for, for months. We turned up at the appointment and just before Kai had a huge seizure and was completely out of it. Wheeling him in they could see for themselves how much I struggled to hold him up right, as he was slumped over the side, and steer at the same time. Kai had woken up and flirted up a storm, lots of eye contact a cheeky "Yeah, baby." in his Jamaican accent and the wheelchair was ordered!

Taking the wheelchair on holiday was going to make my life so much easier, or so I thought. First, we discovered the wheelchair was not great at bumping up and down a kerb, in fact it would get stuck which was dangerous especially as I had the other children with walking with me. The recline position meant the handle bars would lower, quite a lot, I mean I am not tall by any means but even I struggled to bend down to push it. The padding I was excited about was useless, it was padded in all the wrong places and offered no support what so ever when Kai had a huge seizure, which was daily sometimes five times a day. Then we discovered the head support would come very loose and the foot plates were also loose, which luckily Scott managed to fix.

We always included Kai in everything we did, apart from the cinema as for him that was loud, dark and too much for him to handle. We spent every day on the beach which Kai loved. We also brought him a tent, so he could curl up in his cosy position and not get an ear full of sand or sun burn! Chips and ice cream on the beach, picnics in the park, theme parks - we did it all. Kai was loving chips for lunch and dinner every day and the change of scenery did us all the world of good. We felt so lucky and so blessed to all be there together as a few months before we never dreamed Kai would still be here.

This holiday was special, and we made so many memories that I would treasure forever. We also discovered the local beach in West Wittering hired out special sand friendly wheelchairs, this instantly made our life's so much easier! They were free to hire, and we made the most of them going quite a few times that week to the beach. Kai finally got pushed into the sea, although looking back at the pictures makes me laugh as his feet were up in the air! He hated cold water and as he smiled, laughed and waved his little hands, watching him and his dad together made me smile with joy.

I still often sit here now and wish I could rewind time, Lola at my feet building a sand castle, Scott, Bailey, Daisy and Honey-Mae surfing in the sea, and Kai where he always was, with his mum curled up head in my lap. If I could rewind time it would be to that moment, all of us together blissfully unaware at how our lives would soon never be the same again.

***

We decided a trip to Ikea was in order, Scott and I had moved into the smallest room in the house to give the three girls more space. All our clothes were now scattered on our floor as we had no wardrobes that would fit into our tiny little room. We loaded the van up and off we all went, Kai loved it as we obviously stopped for his favourite meal on the way there, a McDonald's.

Once there we walked in to Scott's idea of hell on a Sunday afternoon and walked straight into their new line of chairs. In front of us was a bright mustard coloured seat that we called a throne. Scott's face lit up instantly, "Kai needs that!" he said. It was near on £300, way over our budget. He showed Kai and his face instantly lit up, so it was decided that Kai would have his throne. Finishing up at the store we realised there was no way we were going to fit wardrobes and the chair along with Kai his wheelchair and the other children in the van, so we came home with a new throne! The clothes would have to stay on the floor that bit longer.

Bailey's last day of school came around and I couldn't believe that he would now be in secondary school. I was still questioning if I had done the right thing by putting him into a mainstream school, but with limited choices we felt we had no other option. I shed many tears as he was so fully supported there by his teachers and his amazing SENCO, I struggled to see how he would get on without so much help. I was glad we were going on another holiday, this time to Great Yarmouth, I needed the distraction!

We had an amazing time on holiday, eating candy floss and ice cream until we felt sick. Chips on

50

the beach and late-night arcade journeys. Kai loved every single minute of it, and Scott and I agreed that the following year we would save hard and book another two holidays for him. It's the least all our children deserved. I felt that they had missed out on so much and they rarely complained about it, they accepted that we always had to put Kai's needs before any plans. We also met up with my brother Thomas and his girlfriend Sharlene and my nephew. We went to Petits farm and had a lovely day laughing eating our picnic and going on the little rides.

It was all going so well until Kai's wheelchair, which by now we had been struggling with for so long, decided that this was the perfect moment to cease working. The foot plate and leg rest dropped, it took Scott and Thomas ages trying to put tie wraps and wire around it to hold it back in place. Kai looked at us as if to say, "Well don't expect me to lift my leg the whole way around here." To prove his point, he dragged his foot along the ground stopping the chair from being wheeled completely! In the end they used an old spanner Thomas luckily had in his car and managed to tie it around and raise the footplate off the floor. It lasted for the whole holiday!

We had the best summer, we went to Gulliver's Land and Wicksteed Park with Beckie, Jude and Beckie's mum who we called Dot. Picnics at the local splash park, bowling with Jodie (little mum) and her children. When we got to the bowling alley and they realised we had a wheelchair we were upgraded to VIP which the kids thought was brilliant! Daisy said it was because they knew Kai was a king! Every day we were doing something to make the year before fade away and make new memories, which we now knew were so important. We had family BBQs with my step-mum Terri, my brother Harry and sister Lily-Rose, quad bikes were ridden around the garden, with Kai at the front of course! Pool parties and friends over, it really was the most magical summer and one I will treasure for the rest of my life.

Soon September rolled around, and Bailey went off to secondary school, I was a bag of nerves. I knew that with his autism, Tourette's, ADHD, OCD and anxiety he was an easy target for other children. I also made sure he was told every day he was loved and what a special boy he was. He was kind funny and considerate of others, and rightly or wrongly I had also taught him to never ever hit first. But if he was hit, to hit back, I didn't want him seen as an easy target, and I knew how brutal secondary school could be!

Lola started nursery and I didn't worry once about her! She was the feisty head strong and independent child of ours. If anything, I was scared for her teachers more than for her! She is that one child you cannot ever leave alone - she has smeared Sudocrem into the carpets, ripped wires out of the wall, and terrorised our poor dog, Buddy. I often walk into the front room and find her riding the dog shouting "Yee-ha!". The two other girls were also going up a year, which was scary how fast it was all going! Honey-Mae is the confident headstrong child who will always fight her ground. Kind to others but if she thinks something isn't right she will say it out loud! She is also the double of me, a little mini me in more ways than one, and boy does that girl answer back!

Daisy is very much like Scott, kind sensitive with a heart of gold. She is the quietest out of the three girls. Her and Kai always had the strongest bond, she would curl up in his lap and read him a story or put headphones on him and sit with him listening to music. They always seemed to be sharing an unspoken joke, and I would walk in to find them both asleep in each other's arms, hand in hand. I couldn't believe how fast my babies were all growing up, and I knew that they were better people for having Kai in their life's, as we all were.

Around this time, I started to bleed very heavily, so much so that if I left the house I was worried I would flood through. I was also starting to get crippling headaches that would last for days, they would ease off and then come back. I went to the doctor after much nagging from Scott, Becki and Terri. The doctor took all my bloods and told me to wait for the results. As it turned out I didn't have to wait long, and I was called back in. My doctor said I had zero hormones in my body at all, and if I wanted to get pregnant it would be impossible. That didn't concern me at all as I didn't want any more children - Doctor took all my bloods and told me to wait for the results. As it turned out I didn't have to wait long, and I was called back in. My Doctor said I had zero hormones in my body at all, and if I wanted to get pregnant it would be impossible. That didn't concern me at all as I didn't want any more children, the last couple of years taught me that Kai needed my undivided attention health-wise. He then said that he was almost certain I had a pituitary gland tumour which was why my bloods had come back the way they had. He referred me to a specialist and told me that there would be a chance I would have to have an operation, depending on the size and location. I knew from experience that a referral could take months and so I pushed it to the back of my mind. Why worry about something that could be nothing? Scott's reaction when I told him was as expected, he instantly started to worry and thought of the worst-case scenario. I honestly didn't give it a thought, the only thing worrying me was who would care for Kai if I had to have an operation? Who would take the kids to school or do the shopping?

LOOM BANDS AND HULA HOOPS

Kai's nappies were now full and regular, and I only had to have the community nurses out twice to help him. During one nappy change I lay Kai on the floor and put his legs into the air ready to change him, as I did Honey-Mae shouted, "What is that in his poo?" We all looked down at the half hanging out brightly coloured object when Daisy shouted, "I wondered where my loom band bracelet went!" We all cried with laughter, that boy, no matter how clean and bare my house was, managed to always find something to swallow! On another occasion I was changing Kai and Daisy fell about laughing, Kai had pooped out a "Well done" sticker! "Kai is praising himself Mum," Bailey laughed. The sticker seemed apt for the occasion!

The thing with Kai was he loved his food. It didn't matter if it wasn't his - he would take it off you. If he saw it and he wanted it, then it was his for the taking! I had spent a few minutes showing Lola what everyone once did as children with a packet of Hula Hoops. Kai who had just finished his was sitting next to us watching. I placed a round crisp on each of her fingers and she looked in amazement at them and laughed. "Look Kai, Kai," she shouted waving her little hands in his face. Kai who pretended to look really interested bent over grabbed her hand and sucked them all off in one go. She stood wide eyed not knowing if she should laugh or cry, and I fell about laughing. That was the last time Lola showed Kai her Hula Hoop trick!

My birthday was coming up in a months' time and Scott mentioned taking me away for a weekend. I had only left Kai overnight once before and having babies and being in hospital was the only time we were ever apart. I mentioned it to Beckie and straight away she said "Do it! Book it and I will have Kai. It's not a problem, I would love to have Kai to myself for once!" and so we did. We booked a lovely little annex house in Sussex not far from Brighton. It was a month away yet, so I had plenty of time to worry! Beckie said she would stay at my house with her son Jude and Dot would come. I would leave her with 3 of the children and Terri said she would have the other two, I knew they would be all right and a weekend away would do us the world of good.

Bailey had been at school a couple of weeks when an incident occurred; a few year eight kids had taken it upon themselves to single him out. He was jumped on from behind and punched in the head, while seven others stood around intimidating him. I was livid, but also, I was happy that Bailey hadn't taken it lying down and had fought back. It led to weeks of the same group of children following him around, stealing his bag and hiding it making him late for lessons, and pushing him about. I went in a few times and sent emails stating I was unhappy at the fact Bailey was being bullied in his first few weeks of school. I can't fault the school they did all they could to stop it and for a while things calmed down.

As like any other night Kai stood by the door demanding a bath, he would wander backwards and forwards shouting and complaining, eventually giving you puppy dog eyes and saying "Mum," until I gave in. I shouldn't really have been bathing him, that's what his shower room was for and the shower made it so much easier for me. But Kai loved nothing more than to lay in a bath full of bubbles and splash around happily. I had recently brought him a bath chair to make this easier for him, and me.

Adele and I travelled miles away in the middle of nowhere to pick up one I had found. It had a remote control and it would go all the way up to the top of the bath, you could sit Kai on and swivel his legs around and lower it. This is going to be amazing I thought! No, it was anything but amazing. Kai hated it and made it known by sliding off it as much as he could and defiantly splashed around in the smallest space he could find. I would then have to lift him back on to the seat which made it pointless! I got rid of it and went back to struggling. I tried to make it so I showered him every evening (some days it was mornings too due to a seizure) and bathed him as a treat over the weekend. I ran him a warm bath and he literally flew into it, that was the funny thing about Kai he would quite happily help you when it was what he wanted. He wasn't so helpful when it was something he didn't want, like getting him out of the bath!

As I watched him giggle and splash the girls started to fight in the front room. The front room is right next to the bathroom, and as I looked Lola was threatening to throw things at the girls. Remote controls, books and toys were being launched at them while they screamed trying to hide from her. Scott was at work, so I ran into the living room took the toys off her and told her off. I was gone seconds and as I ran back into the bathroom Kai was starting to have a seizure. This was no ordinary seizure, his whole body was twisting and jerking and thrashing around. His head was going under the water and I tried desperately to get a grip of him before his whole head was submerged. I couldn't get a grip of him at all, he was too slippery, and his seizure was so strong, I managed to lift his head up and keep it up out of the water. Then gathering all my strength, I looped my arms under his and wrenched him from the bath. I rolled him on his side and smacked his back as hard as I could while he coughed and spluttered. My heart was racing as I checked him over, he was now in his deep sleep breathing fine. I was worried he could have aspirated on the water, although not much got into his lungs as I managed to keep his head from going under, he did swallow some. I carried him into the living room and rang for an ambulance as I dried and dressed him ready for a trip to hospital. The girls ran around packing him a bag in case he had to stay overnight. I felt so guilty that my children had seen all they had in their short lives. No child should know how to deal with a seizure or pack for an emergency bag.

The ambulance came out and although Kai's observations were fine they too wanted him to be observed. Bailey instantly got upset and demanded to come to the hospital with me, and Scott stayed at home with the girls. After hours of checks and tests Kai was able to come home. We got home in the middle of the night and as usual if I was worried about Kai I would sleep with him. Sometimes getting into his bed with him for a snuggle, or I would sleep on a pull-out bed on the floor. Scott would also sleep in with us as he said it wasn't fair he slept in a comfy bed on his own. We often had little sleepovers in Kai's room, even if it was just to ease my mind after a bad seizure or a dreadful day. Although, with the video camera now I had much more peace of mind. I knew that from now on Kai wouldn't be able to have a bath, which really upset me. One of Kai's main pleasures in life was a bath and now seizures had also stolen that from him. I couldn't help but feel angry and bitter, I could deal with everything that was thrown at us, but Kai's seizures were one thing I found hard to come to terms with. It seemed the older he got the worse they became and the more frightened I got that this could be the one that killed him.

The decking company ATG got in touch and measured up the garden and talked us through what the decking would look like for Kai. I was so happy that this would now be so much safer for Kai and he would have an amazing summer next year out of the sun he hated so much! They made a start that week and would work through the weekend we were away.

October came around and Scott and I were going away for one of our first weekends alone together. I was so nervous, although I knew Beckie was more than capable and I wouldn't ever leave Kai with anyone else I still worried. Kai used to go on hunger strike if I went out and would play Scott and Beckie up. I used to come home and feed him while he looked cross that I dared leave his side. Secretly I loved it, that's how close we were, even food couldn't win over Kai's love for his mum. Beckie had Lola, Bailey and Kai, and Terri had Honey-Mae and Daisy. I knew they would all be fine, but as any mum knows too well you still worry and feel guilty! Baileys OCD was also on a whole new level now, he wouldn't eat anything not prepared by me, Scott or Beckie. If we went out he would only eat pre-made packaged food or things cooked with gloves on. I knew at least he would eat if I left him with Beckie!

We packed our bags and drove the couple of hours trip to a village just outside Brighton for my birthday weekend that Scott told me would be one I would never forget. We had so much fun just the two of us, carefree walking arm in arm along the beach. We spent the whole first day shopping where Scott treated me to so many new clothes I felt like Vivian from Pretty Woman! Of course, I checked in on the kids, Kai more than any of them and in the end Beckie told me he was fine and to piss off and have fun. We went to the cinema to see IT and ate until our bellies hurt. We had meals out, and ice-creams on the beach, we brought as many snacks as we could and watched TV late into the night knowing we didn't have to get up early the next day. We had the most amazing weekend and I fell deeper in love with Scott, even though that felt like it wasn't possible.

We talked about our fears, our dreams of travelling the world in a converted camper van with Kai and buying a chalet to convert and rent out to families like ours that struggled. We came home feeling refreshed relaxed and worry free. I got home to full-on hugs and thank you's for the gifts we had brought the kids. Straight away I smothered Kai in big kisses and he seemed so pleased to see us. Beckie then told me, "I lied when I said Kai was fine, the little sod went on sleep strike the whole first night, he was up shouting 'Mum' angrily all night!" My face must have said it all as Beckie said "Well if I would have told you, you would have only worried and come home and he was fine the next night!" She was right, I would have!

The decking was now complete, and I couldn't wait for Kai to come home from school and see it! We were over the moon with what Hailey and her sister in law and the charity had done for us. We now had a ramp for Kai's wheelchair and railings all the way around, so Kai couldn't just step off and fall. Also, a huge fitted shelter that I planned to buy a big rattan sofa bed and chair and table set for Kai to lay on and enjoy for his 16th birthday in January. Kai came home from school and I fed him first and then Scott led him through his room and straight out of his patio doors onto his very own decking. Daisy was standing shouting "Look Kai! This is all for you! It's all yours!" and at that exact moment Kai broke into the biggest cheesiest grin ever that showed pure delight. It is one of my favourite photos of Kai ever, standing there care free so happy on his very own decking area.

Kai's seizures were now through the roof, I had videoed many to show the consultants exactly what Kai went through during one. Although, still not as many as he used to have before his third and final brain operation they were stronger and lasting longer. Kai could be smiling one minute then crashing through the air the next. He often had facial injuries even while wearing his helmet. The school were also concerned and had to phone an ambulance several times over the next two months. Kai would out stretch his arms, and then violently fall. He would then thrash around, head butting the floor repeatedly or most recently punching himself in the face repeatedly mid seizure. It was so hard to stop this as his limbs were rigid mid-seizure and I was scared of hurting him, so I would place my hand between his face and fist so he would punch me and not his face. I got a call from the school one day that an ambulance had been called as Kai had a seizure and wasn't responding after. I raced to the school with a car full of shopping and beat the ambulance there. Scott and Terri also met me at the school. Kai went into hospital and was observed but was then sent home. All Kai's saturations were fine and as scary as it was for us to watch and to see, he always came around after. He started having them more at home too, and again the coming around phase was taking longer each time. It frightened me as although he was still breathing he went completely blue, even his ears. He would let out a scream, have his seizure, and then be flat out for hours. This would make it impossible to leave the house or move him a lot of the time. I would have to change his urine-soaked clothes and nappy while he was completely out of it.

Ambulances for Kai was becoming a regular occurrence and I decided to buy a SATS machine with my friend Paula's guidance. This would then settle the school's mind as well as my own, as it would check his heart rate and oxygen levels. If they fell below a certain number, then I and the school would know that an ambulance was needed. While this was on its way to me Kai again had another huge seizure at school. I was at home really ill with tonsillitis and could hardly stand as I was aching from head to toe. The school phoned me, and I felt terrible that I couldn't get there fast enough to see if Kai was ok. I phoned Beckie in tears as I couldn't get hold of Scott, who was working. Straight away she left work and went to Kai's school to wait for the ambulance. She kept in contact with me for the next half hour. By this point I was driving myself mad and wanted to be with Kai, so I took a handful of painkillers and rushed to the school. By the time I had got there Beckie was smiling, she explained they were just about to take Kai when she said let me see if I can wake him. She sat him up and asked him if he wanted a drink and he opened his eyes! When I saw him, he looked exhausted but was alert and awake and I took him home with me, where we spent the day feeling sorry for ourselves cuddled up on the sofa.

After kicking off and screaming and shouting, my appointment came through for a different consultant locally to us as Dr James couldn't see us until January. I had high hopes and hoped this consultant would be as understanding and helpful as Dr James was with us. I had no faith in many consultants and a lot of them hated me. I had a feeling I was pre-judged as I look a lot younger than I am, and if I questioned anything or refused I was made to feel like I didn't know what I was doing. I knew my son more than anyone in this world and if I didn't agree with something I would argue until I was blue in the face. This often didn't go down very well. I also felt resentful that a lot of them didn't seem to have a clue about Kai and some of their input I felt was guess work. I had tried every drug possible for Kai, one made him zombified, another made him sleep too much, or not enough. There was one with which he would spend the day crying which upset me as Kai never cried. I wasn't keen on introducing new drugs for Kai without speaking to Dr James first as I trusted him, this didn't always go down too well. We went through three types of surgery for Kai and although they reduced his seizures they never took them away, and they would come back with vengeance.

The last appointment I had with Dr James I had asked him about CBD oil and if I could try Kai with it. I had read up a lot on the benefits of cannabis oil which seemed to reduce many seizures in people with epilepsy. I had high hopes for it possibly working for Kai, but I also wasn't stupid I knew that as with any drugs there were risks. I would never put Kai on CBD oil without medical support and back up which people found hard to understand. The side effects Dr James told me were not known as such yet as they were still trialling it, but he did know it could reduce or increase appetite. What with Kai having lost so much weight I didn't want to risk him losing any more as he couldn't afford to. We both decided that once Kai had gained another stone we could re-evaluate CBD oil. At present there was only limited spaces on the trial and Kai wouldn't be a candidate yet due to his weight. I understood and agreed completely, although Kai was on his way to weighing eight stone now he still was very slender as he was 5ft 5" tall. I also knew from research that putting Kai on CBD oil alongside his medication he was on, like Clobozam, could be very dangerous. Regular blood tests would be needed to keep an eye on Kai and I knew without medical back up there was no way we would try CBD oil. We agreed that we would talk about it more in six months' time.

I instantly took a dislike to Kai's new local consultant - she had that look that I hated on her face, one of sympathy. I could never understand that look, yes Kai was disabled, yes it was bloody challenging work especially when you had no outside help. But no, I didn't want sympathy, this boy was to me my entire world. He made the sun shine with his smile, he made every day worth getting up for. He made me laugh and appreciate the silliest things in life. She started off asking lots of questions and going over his background. Kai sat oblivious in his chair head in his hands with a bored expression on his face. I asked why Kai's bowels had just suddenly stopped working as they should in the first place, and she told me it was common in children with disabilities and just one of those things. That pissed me off instantly - why now? Kai's diet was so varied now compared to years ago when he would only eat bland coloured food. He now ate a variety of fruit, veg and dinners. I felt like her answer was a cop out, and a lazy-arsed excuse. She then went on to say what a marvellous job I was doing and how Kai must be such a burden on me and us as a family. I had to grip my chair to stop me from punching her straight in her face. Anger bubbled inside me and I switched off after that. This woman was clueless and was going to be no benefit to us at all; I decided there and then that this would be the last time I would turn up at her appointments. She went on to say had I signed a DNR yet? I asked to her to repeat the question. DNR? What the hell was she talking about? The only DNR I knew was a do not resuscitate form. Why in the world would I need to sign one of those? She explained that often it was asked of families to have one in place for the future in case anything was to happen. It was sometimes kinder to let their child go. I was speechless and told her over my dead body would I ever sign such a form. Why the hell was she asking me to sign one or have one in place when Kai was fine? His bowels were great now and he was gaining weight. I told her I would never sign that form, and she said we could talk about it the next time I saw her. I never did see her again.

I was becoming more and more frustrated with the lack of help, and our social worker who we had for a couple of months took us off her books. Apparently, we were not a family in need and didn't require their help, how they came to that conclusion I will never know. I had made it known I was struggling physically and yet we were still signed off. We were put on the short breaks team's books instead, which really didn't seem like it would help much at all. We were visited at home by a lovely guy from the short breaks team who met Kai and instantly liked him. He could see what a big boy he was and how I was struggling and was very helpful with giving us his time to advise us, but I knew it would all come down to red tape and criteria again. He asked what kind of help we wanted, I replied that having someone to come in on weekday mornings would be a major help as it took me hours getting Kai ready before I even started on the other four children. He said I would have to advertise for this myself which I did, but it led to nothing. The hours I wanted weren't suitable for anyone; I wanted an hour a day from 7-8am, Monday to Friday. I really didn't think I was asking for much! According to the professionals this would be hard to achieve as we had no equipment for Kai, and I would need two people and equipment. Of course, their health and safety came first, I felt like screaming but I have been doing this alone for years! Where was the concern for my health and safety? Why were we sixty-two in the queue for a hoist! I felt and still do to this day feel that it is made nearly almost impossible for anyone to receive any kind of help at all, and it makes me sick to my stomach to think of others struggling. I explained that our weekends were now affected, and we couldn't do much together as Scott worked Saturdays, I no longer had Beckie's help and Kai would often have a seizure that would result in him sleeping a lot. He mentioned an inclusion group, which anyone who knows me knows would have been a big deal for me to consider this. But, I also had my other children to think of and agreed that Kai being picked up to go on a day trip on a Saturday with other children his age would be perfect for him, and us. I could then take the kids out while Kai was in capable hands enjoying himself. I swallowed my pride and said yes, the decision came back that Kai didn't meet the criteria. This bloody criteria that no one had ever seen or bloody spoken of in depth was putting a major strain on me!

OUR LAST CHRISTMAS
2018

Christmas time was fast approaching, and I couldn't wait! It always had been my favourite time of year. We brought a brand-new tree and filled it with lots of decorations. Presents were wrapped, and a huge shop was done to prepare for the week of hibernating. The previous Christmas we had a big family one, I had never spent it with Terri or my brothers or sisters. So, we had Terri, Georgia Harry, Lily-Rose and Sheila over. It was a lovely Christmas full of great memories! This year, though, was going to be a quiet one, just the seven of us. We had gone all out, getting the kids everything, they wanted and some extras. They all had a scooter each as well as their main presents. We got Kai a new trampoline for the garden which he spent most of his time asleep on more than bouncing! The children had taken it in turns to be ill the week before Christmas, all of them except for Kai. I was hoping we would wake up to an illness free house in the morning! Beckie came around with Jude as she always does on Christmas Eve. We would do our traditional present swapping a day early so we could see the children's faces and had a McDonald's meal. The kids also had their traditional Christmas Eve boxes with new pyjamas, hot chocolate and a Christmas DVD, along with some snacks. In the evening we always ordered a pizza and the kids would be buzzing from excitement and over eating junk food!

This Christmas we also learnt that I in fact didn't have a pituitary gland tumour after all. The relief to Scott was immense. He was worried sick, I really wasn't at all. I was relieved that it was behind us and I didn't have to worry about childcare and driving the kids about now. I had come off the contraceptive pill and after further tests my hormones had started to rise on their own, the headaches also stopped, but the bleeding remained the same, so I was advised to go for a smear test, which I did. I now just had to wait and see what was going on with this body of mine!

Christmas morning came around and all the kids slept in! It was me running around waking them all up in excitement. The look of joy on their faces when they opened the living room door and saw presents all over the living room floor was priceless! They started tearing at them while we recorded it all, and then I went in to get Kai up. I had now become so much better after my counselling and explaining to Scott about my fears, and I was fine to go into Kai's room now. The fear hadn't left me, but I felt like I could manage it now. Night times were still really bad, I would constantly check Kai's monitor and lay awake panicking, but I felt like I had it all under control now, I had finally been honest and spoken out. I still took my beta blockers and they were helping me a lot. Kai was fast asleep, and I shook him awake, he opened one eye and looked at me as if to say, "Oh piss off woman!" so I gave him his meds and left his door open, I would let him have a bit longer!

Kai didn't roll out of his bed until 10.00am, and even that was under duress! I gave him some breakfast and got him changed ready to open his presents. He got a lovely elf hat from his teachers at school and I put it on him. He looked so pissed off we called him an angry elf all day while he sat unamused at all the fuss and noise! Even Christmas dinner wasn't exciting Kai like it usually did and he hardly touched his food. Instead he curled up on the sofa while I checked his temperature, it was slightly raised, and I knew he had picked up the dreaded bug. He managed to eat a few snacky bits and some pudding but didn't seem to be himself, I dosed him up and snuggled up to him. Scott and I would be sleeping in his room tonight!

Boxing Day and Kai was no better, he was full of snot and I had been checking on him next to me throughout the night. He just wanted to sleep and his temperate was creeping up throughout the day. By the afternoon you could see his little red rimmed heavy eyes and his runny nose and see how fed up he was. I kept a close eye on him and again we shared his room with him that night. The following day Kai looked dreadful, he wasn't getting any better and his temperature was still raised even after medication. I always worried when it came to Kai and ended up in tears as he wouldn't eat a thing. I instantly worried he would start to lose weight that we'd struggled so hard to get back onto him. He just lay and slept all day, and I phoned the out of hours doctor who agreed, after my refusal to lift him and bring him to the surgery, to come out and see us. Kai's chest and throat, etc, was clear but the doctor was equally concerned. He decided to give Kai antibiotics anyway as he said this looked like a nasty bug. Kai hadn't been this unwell for ages! All the other children were constantly picking up bugs, but Kai was hardly ever ill, and if he was he was also the last one to get it! We often joked it was because his tummy was cast iron, I mean everything that boy had eaten that he shouldn't have over the years! The doctor said we were to get the prescription and start them right away. It was now 9.00 at night two days after Christmas! So, me and the girl's, still in our pyjamas, went to Asda to get Kai's meds, we joked we would never leave the house looking the state we did for anyone else!

We slept with Kai for the whole week and completed his antibiotics, he was still very quiet and not eating much at all. I was now giving him three milkshakes crammed with as many calories as I could fit in them! This seemed to work as when he recovered we weighed him, and he didn't lose a single pound! I was gutted Kai was so poorly over Christmas, he loved the food and over indulging we did. I said to Scott, "next year we will make it up to him." If only that was the case.

January was a busy month, we had lots of hospital appointments and I had to apply for PIP as DLA was now going to be changed over as Kai would be turning 16 on the 21st January. I couldn't believe it had come around so quickly and was very emotional. We also had to get used to the fact that Kai would be moving over to adult care by the end of 2018 and losing all his consultants I had grown to trust. This year was going to be a very testing year, I knew how adult care worked after seeing my mum so ill and I didn't hold out much hope. I was particularly upset that this would mean we wouldn't be seeing Dr James anymore, I had told him that he would have to see us as I wouldn't trust anyone else!

The PIP forms were a nightmare and I felt resentful that I had to prove that Kai had a lifelong condition that would never get any better. I gathered a huge box full of his last two years of hospital stays and visits and planned to send them in with the form! We had a home visit from a lady from PIP to prove that I had to sign and take care of the paperwork, not Kai. This seemed like madness to me and a complete waste of time! I couldn't believe the extra stress put on families by PIP, just to prove why you still needed to claim disability money. We were seen at GOSH who were pleased with Kai's progress with his bowels, and they made an appointment for the following December, which was when we would be moved into adult care. The thought of not having a hospital like GOSH as an option made me feel sick to my stomach.

The children all went back to school, the decorations came down and Christmas was now over.

I told the school about Kai being ill at Christmas and he seemed a lot better in himself now and was eating normally again. Seizure-wise he was not doing too great at all, and we had an appointment in January with Dr James, and another one in January with his local bowel team. Kai continued having horrendous seizures at school, and at home. He was still taking a long time to come around afterwards and was non-responsive. I felt a little better having his SATS monitor to check that he was ok. One night, Kai had a huge seizure in the shower as he stood up out of his chair. As he was naked and covered in soap, I tried to catch him, but he slipped straight through my hands and landed with a whack on the floor banging his head and back. I felt terrible, especially when he did the exact same thing to Scott two days later in the shower. We now had to make sure he was sitting down to be rinsed off as usually liked to stand and feel the water running all over him and would, most of the time, refuse to sit in his chair. He would make his whole body go rigid and be as difficult as he could!

The appointments came around quickly and after a thorough examination of his bowels Kai was declared free from any blockage! I felt like we could take on the world! We had done it, together and with some outside help we had kept his bowels clear for nearly a year now! Kai's weight was doing lovely too, and when he was measured I found out he was now 5ft 6", he loved that, standing over me and Scott laughing at our smallness! I felt like I was walking on air, Kai was clear health wise, now we had to tackle his seizures and I knew we had an appointment with

Dr James in two days' time. I was determined to keep fattening Kai up and get him on to the cannabis oil.

At home, I was sitting on the sofa with Kai when he suddenly went quiet, his face turned into a little grin and his eyes went smaller. I instantly recognised this as an absence seizure. He had three little ones in a row and I said to Scott instantly "I don't like that one bit." Scott reassured me as I worked myself up, yes, he had always had absence seizures but not for a while, and as he had had three in a row I instantly worried it would lead to a more aggressive seizure. The next few nights I had his monitor right next to me and hardly slept as I checked him throughout the night. He didn't have any more over the next few days, but it didn't stop me from worrying and checking on him constantly.

Dr James was great as usual and watched the videos I had been taking of Kai during a seizure. He also agreed that Kai's seizures were uncontrollable now and advised me to try Kai on a new medication, but to put him on the new medication he would have to be weaned off the one he was already on. We spoke about Kai transitioning to adult care and he laughed when I said we wouldn't be leaving and does any adult still see him? as if not Kai would be the first to do so! Dr James always complimented me on how well I was doing, how well I seemed to be managing Kai and how outraged he was that we had no support in place. He too felt that Kai now needed outside help in the mornings and told me that we had a right to this as a family. He also told me he would be sending angry emails to the relevant people to back up our pleas for some outside support. We left the appointment with an agreement to meet him sooner to see how Kai was getting on with his medication and talk through the next step. I secretly hoped that this would be the appointment that would change Kai's life, maybe we would be able to get him on the oil that I had seen so many satisfactory results with.

A standard hospital appointment always ended with Kai having a McDonald's or a Burger king meal. This time it was Burger King, and I plonked a crown on his head and took lots of pictures of Kai, Lola and myself having a celebratory lunch. He didn't look impressed in any of them and gave a look as if to say "Really? Another photo?" We also walked around the shops in the hospital and chose Daisy a Worry Monster teddy for her upcoming birthday in March. Kai kept looking at the brightly pink coloured one so that's the one we went with. You unzipped its mouth and popped in your written down worries and the monster ate them as you slept. I knew that Daisy would love it, especially as Kai had input in choosing it.

AND THEN THE SNOW FELL...

Friday the 19th January is the date that will forever be etched in my mind, as it was my last day with my boy. I hadn't been feeling great and Scott was off work feeling just as rough as me. Both achy and drained and the weather mimicked how we felt. Scott felt so poorly he was laid out on the sofa in a quilt and couldn't get warm. I still had things to do around the house. Kai's 16th birthday was coming up in two days' time, it was also Jude's birthday on the very same day. Beckie had planned a big party for Jude in the hall, and we always went to his parties, this year however as it was Kai's 16th we had booked him a table at Frankie & Benny's. The kids were so excited; we had a huge chocolate cake ordered by The Cakey Lady, who had made Kai's previous cakes. I knew she would go all out and had asked for as much chocolate as possible topped with his name and a crown and a big number 16. I had brought Kai lots of his favourite clothes he felt cosiest in - Puma hoodies and tracksuit bottoms, and aftershave and a razor set. I had finally given in and knew that Kai would now have to be regularly shaved, as much as I had kidded myself it was a chocolate moustache and not hairs! A lovely cushion to go with his throne in his room and a few other bits. His main present I was ordering once the weather was brighter was a huge chair set for his decking. I knew Kai would love to have a big rattan bed with a cover over it, so he could lay his lazy bum down on and sleep the hot days away. I had picked out the chair and table set with Scott, who also agreed we shouldn't order it yet as it would only sit in the garage for a few months. I busied myself with going to the town and buying wrapping paper and cards and a 16th birthday candle. I spent the morning wrapping Kai's presents and the afternoon preparing his dinner for when he got home.

I picked the kids up from school and was chatting to the mums in the playground about how when I saw them next I would be a mum of a 16-year-old! I felt very emotional about it and was so proud that Kai had beaten all his battles and was here to celebrate another year. Scott, Beckie and I had spoken the previous year about us all going away together to Disneyland for Kai's 16th. We never got around to organising or saving for it, but knew we wanted to do that in the future. This birthday meant so much to everyone who was close to Kai as they knew what a big milestone it was to us all.

All the way home the kids talked about how they would help Kai open all his presents, what pudding they would order at the restaurant and what cake I had got him this year. We all got home and was happy to shut the door on the bitterly, wintery weather we were having. Kai soon came home from school and as usual he wouldn't talk to me until he was fed his dinner! He had hot dogs and chips and wolfed the lot down followed by a big chocolate bar and a milkshake. I decided that as I'd had such a busy day I would shower and bath all the kids in the morning. I was achy and tired as I hadn't slept properly the last few nights due to Kai having his absence seizures, I had checked on him and lay awake worrying. The tiredness was now catching up with me and I knew we had a busy weekend ahead of us. Kai must have sensed this and kept me on his toes all evening, climbing and stamping on his dad who was shivering under a quilt. He kept wandering up to Scott and trying to dribble on him, which I found hilarious! We both told Kai off and he loved it! He did it more and was holding his belly crying of laughter at our mocked angry voices. He jumped on the kids and kicked the dog on his way into the kitchen to look for more mischief! He kept going next to the bathroom door and shouting "Mum," because he wanted a bath. Something I hadn't been able to do since his seizure in the bath a few months back. I told him I would bath him as a birthday treat over the weekend and continued to tell him off in my playful angry voice. This made him laugh harder.

Soon it was the children's bed time and on his way to his room Kai stood at the glass cake holder I had and reached out for a cake. The stand used to fascinate him, he used to stand for ages trying to work out how he could see all these cakes but couldn't touch them. It was cute to watch, and I

79

chuckled as I ushered him into his room. "You have had a cake, Kai Hammond, you little pig, you are not having anymore." He climbed into bed and laughed at my voice. I gave him a kiss on his lips as I tucked him under his Danger Mouse quilt. I stood stroking the outline of his face as I did every night. Whispering how much I loved him, how he was a special boy and Mummy's little Peter Pan. How lucky I was never to have to worry about sharing him with anyone, he was all mine. He looked back up at me his eyes reflecting the thousands of unspoken words he wanted to say and gave me a grin. "See you in the morning my beautiful boy," I said. As I closed the door of his bed, I never knew that was the last time I would see my boy's beautiful blue eyes and his big cheeky smile.

I watched some TV with Scott and we both started to get ready for bed, I walked to check on Kai and could hear him signing his own song at 11.30pm. I smiled, as did Scott, and we both went up to bed. I put Kai's monitor on and fell into a deep sleep. Both Scott and I woke up at 5.00am and went to the toilet, something we never usually do. We were both going to check on Kai but decided against it as he was sound asleep, and we didn't want to wake him up as this would always cause a seizure. I climbed back in bed and fell straight back to sleep, I must have needed it, as I didn't wake up until 7.00am. The girls and Bailey were already downstairs not long getting up before me. Kai was quiet, so I sorted the kids out keeping an eye on the time. Kai could never go more than an hour over his medication time, so I decided to leave him in bed until 8.00am and let him have a little lay in. I pottered about doing some house work, while the kids finished breakfast and sat watching TV.

"Right Mr Hammond, you have had long enough in that bed you lazy boy." I said as I walked into Kai's room. I opened his bed doors and looked down, as I thought Kai was fast asleep still. I chuckled to myself and then did a double take. Kai was in his cosy position as he always slept, bum in the air, knees to his chin and hands next to his head. Only this time Kai's face was buried so deep into his pillow you couldn't see his face at all. Everything stood still, I stood looking but not really talking in what I was seeing. How is he breathing like that? I thought to myself. I could see Kai's ear was very blue from the side, almost purple. My body took over as my mind tried to reason with itself. I gripped Kai under both his arms and pulled him out of bed, as I did so I noticed blood on his pillow, I pulled him up and as I did so I heard him gasp, thank god! I thought to myself. I pulled him out and onto the floor – CPR, CPR, CPR was all I could think as my heart beat so fast I thought it would pound out of my chest. My body felt icy cold as I struggled to take it all in and try to calm myself down enough to give Kai CPR. I lay him on his back and went straight into giving him CPR, I was kneeling with my face to his, when I saw him for the first time. My mind was screaming "He's dead," as the other half of me argued with it, of course he is not dead, this is Kai. Kai always pulls through, this is a dream.

As I looked at Kai again I fell backwards in shock. His eyes were shut tight, his tongue was slightly hanging out of his mouth and he had bit it.

81

My beautiful singing boy was now strangely quiet, I sat staring at him not believing this was real. My mind struggled to find ways to talk itself out of this and to reassure myself. I tried to get up, but my legs wouldn't work, I fell straight back down and had to try to crawl to reach Scott. I was hurrying as fast as I could before falling and crawling trying to get back to my feet. I made it to my feet and looked behind me. Kai was laying on his back and I properly took in what my mind had tried to shut out, Kai was still in his cosy position but now on is back, all his limbs were rigid. His face was blue, I started to scream as the reality kicked in.

The kids all came running and I couldn't talk, I couldn't move, I couldn't walk, I fell to the floor screaming again, a look of panic flashed over their faces as they raced up stairs to get Scott. I later found out they had told Scott I had hurt my leg, as they saw I couldn't walk, and had assumed this was why. Panic set in again before the sane part of my brain wrestled with it as it screamed "Go back, go back and resuscitate him!" I crawled back to Kai hoping for some kind of movement, that I'd made some kind of mistake, but there was none. I put my mouth to his to resuscitate him, and again fell backwards. I sat back up and shook him "Kai, Kai." I was screaming his name, his touch didn't feel warm anymore, he felt like nothing I had ever felt before. I crawled to the bedroom door as I struggled to make sense of everything. A pain like I had never felt came through my heart and took over my body from my head to my toes, and I let out a howl I had never heard before. All my pain rushed out of my mouth as I screamed and howled to get the pain out of me.

The kids all came rushing back in to see me as I was screaming, howling and crying that Kai was dead. The sounds I was making didn't sound like they were coming from me and I couldn't form any words properly. I didn't even think to shut the door and watched one by one as each of my children took in the scene around them, watching their lives' shatter one by one as they each dropped to the floor howling.

Looking back now that is my biggest regret in life, I should have shut the door and not let them see the image of their brother like that. In that moment I couldn't even stand up and didn't even think to do anything to protect them. Scott ran past them shouting "What have you done to your leg?" I was howling and rocking and trying to talk. "Vikki, talk to me where have you hurt your leg?" Scott stood shouting with a look of panic across his face. "He's dead, he's dead, he's dead." I screamed back at him. Scott looked shocked trying to make sense of what I was saying and then he looked behind me. I watched as he fell to his knees screaming, shaking Kai, trying to make it better like he always did. I will never forget his face when he looked up at me, we knew there was no fixing anything this time.

That part of my day on 20th January 2018, one day short of Kai's 16th birthday, is the only part I can recall from my memory. I remember parts, it's like the old-fashioned cinema reel, where the film cuts in and out and goes blank and then back into focus again. I remember managing to get to my feet and stumbling while screaming at the kids to come in the front room. I managed to tell Scott to get Alan from next door, and I picked up the phone and dialled 999 on auto pilot. I couldn't talk and again was just howling and screaming down the phone, which I then threw into a corner of the room. Scott was throwing clothes on and ran to Alan, who was already hanging out of his window after hearing our cries. "Is everything ok, Scott? Do you need me to come over?" Alan asked. Scott stopped running and looked at him, then put his head in his hands and said, "Its Kai, Alan, he's dead."

I remember wanting Beckie and Terri here, I remember calling them, but no words would form. All I could do was wail and cry down the phone, shouting he's dead. Again, I threw the phone and just sank to my knees howling in a ball of pain. Alan came running through, and as soon as I saw him a wave of calm washed over me. It would be ok, Alan had saved him before, he could do it again. I sat waiting and Alan came back out of Kai's room with that same haunted expression we all had. I don't remember any words being spoken, we just looked at each other and I knew then, Kai was dead. It was real.

This is where I can't remember anything more, I don't know if my mind has shut it out, if I went into shock, or maybe it was both. Alan took the children next door, and Dot and Rose (Beckie's mum and aunt arrived). I don't remember words being spoken I just remember screaming and howling and fiercely rocking, wishing for the pain to go away. Beckie arrived, as did the police and ambulance, it seemed like one minute I was alone and the next my house was full of people. I couldn't take it in and to this day I don't remember a thing about the ambulance men, I don't remember Beckie there, I was in a complete trance and couldn't control my body at all. I felt as if everything hurt, I felt so weak and full of despair, rage, anger and denial. I only remember one kind policeman's face, I was still in my Mr Men pyjamas rocking and howling and then I would go silent. The pain would wash back over me again and I would scream and howl. He came over to me and knelt beside me. He pulled my face up to his and said "Vikki, I am so sorry." I stopped for a moment and just stared at him. "I killed him." I shouted, "This is all my fault, I slept through the one night he needed me the most, you need to arrest me." They were the first words I had spoken, while Scott was trying to comfort me, as well as the policeman. I lost it again and was howling "I'm sorry, I am so sorry." Over, and over again until my throat hurt and my voice began to crack.

The policeman sat with me through it all, I don't remember the words he was saying to me, I almost completely blacked out and sat in a trance. I heard the ambulance men talk to the policeman, but I couldn't make out what was being said. The kind policeman looked at me and said, "We are taking Kai to the hospital now, Vikki." My heart skipped a beat and I was snapped out of my trance. A huge surge of relief and hope surged through me, I smiled and sat up. "Is he ok? Will they make him better?" My mind was still trying to kid itself that Kai was fine, hospitals always made Kai better so why couldn't they this time?" The policeman looked at me with tears in his eyes and shook his head, all the hope vanished, and the pain hit me with such force it took my breath away. My mind was spinning, you stupid bitch, you slept while your son was dying, you did this, why did you give him a pillow? How did you not hear him? The thoughts were so fierce and so raw I couldn't control them, and I lost it. I started screaming a high-pitched scream, smashing my head against the drawers, pulling my hair out, punching myself, biting myself. "I killed him." I kept screaming as the policeman calmly tried to soothe me. I sagged down screaming and exhausted I just wanting to be with my boy.

***

A note from Beckie

Saturday the 20th January, the day before our boys 16th and 5th birthdays and also the day that changed our lives forever. I had arranged a big party for Jude with a magician and forty of his friends and family. Vikki had plans of her own with Kai, a meal out and maybe his favourite, swimming. We were going to be doing something together today, maybe bowling and eating out. That morning I got up as normal and gave Jude his breakfast, I jumped in the shower and asked Steve to get Jude ready for football, all very normal. As I was getting dressed my phone rang around 8.20am, Steve called out to let me know it was Vikki phoning. I answered the phone to be met with screams, Vikki was screaming "Kai is dead." Over, and over again. (I still hear her screams to this day). I couldn't get her to listen to me as she just kept on screaming. Steve was looking at me asking, "What is wrong?" with Vikki still on the phone. I answered, "She is saying Kai is dead." He told me to get dressed and go to her, with panic running through me I put the phone down. I threw on some clothes, saying to Steve as I did "I am sure Kai is fine, I bet he's had a seizure and is unresponsive, Kai has done this before." Steve looked at me and said, "Just go, I will take Jude to football."

On the drive to Vikki's I rang my Mum, telling her what had happened and asked if she could meet me there straight away. Just in case I was needed at the hospital with Scott and Vikki, and she could sit with the children. "Of course, but I think I will bring Auntie Rose with me." After speaking to my Mum, I rang my Auntie Rose, explaining again what had happened. Straight away she said, "I will get ready and wait for Mum." Both my Mum and Aunts voices were very calm, I think they thought the same as me, Kai was fine and was unresponsive. Still feeling very panicked driving towards Vikki's I rang my niece Michaela, we spoke until I arrived at Vikki's.

Upon arriving I could see an ambulance, a rapid response car and police cars, Alan was walking up his drive hand in hand with Lola and Daisy (Honey-Mae and Bailey were already there). Alan pointed for me to park on his driveway, as I got out of the car he put his head down. I remember saying "Please, tell me it's not true." He put his arm around me and said, "I am so sorry." I ran into Vikki's to find her curled up on the sofa rocking backwards and forwards. The noise she was making was something I had never heard before, it was almost like an out of body experience. A paramedic was with her trying to comfort her. I sat next to her and wrapped my arms around her, she just kept screaming and shouting, "I want my boy back." The paramedic explained she had phoned for the out of hours GP as she felt Vikki needed some help. Vikki kept saying, "I just want to die, I want to kill myself, I want to be with Kai." I agreed with the paramedic.

Scott was standing in the kitchen talking to the police, I didn't go through, the fear running through my body wouldn't allow me. I stayed with Vikki, I didn't have any words. I just held her as I listened to her screaming, knowing this time I couldn't make it better, as much as I wanted to take her pain away, I couldn't. Around half an hour later I walked outside to call Steve, when I saw my mum and Auntie Rose walking towards me from next door. Mum's eyes were red, and I could see she had been crying, we didn't speak, we both sobbed as she held me. I knew I had to see the children, I slowly walked to Alan and Julie's house thinking what am I going to say? How am I going to make this better? I was greeted by Julie who was stood in the hallway crying, Lola was playing with Corina. Daisy, Honey-Mae and Bailey were sat on the sofa, their little faces were etched with sadness, they just looked at me as I knelt in front of them. Taking their little hands in mine I told them how much I loved them, and I would do anything and everything I could to get them through this.

Back at Vikki and Scott's the paramedics were preparing to take Kai to the hospital, they came through and asked if we wanted to see him to say goodbye before they left. I knew I couldn't see my beautiful boy, I was so scared and frightened that he wouldn't look peaceful. I later apologised to Vikki, who told me she was glad I hadn't seen him like that. My aunt said her goodbyes and she kissed his cheek and told him to sleep tight, she said how beautiful he looked. Because of Kai's age a parent had to go with him, Scott knew Vikki couldn't go and he went, arranging for his brothers to meet him at the hospital.

The house fell into silence, just Vikki, Mum and myself, I remember looking at Mum and saying, "What are we going to do?" She quietly responded, "I don't know, Beckie." She always had an answer or a reassuring word, but not this time. Mum and I were in the kitchen when Vikki walked through and said, "I am having a shower." She was only in there seconds when she walked out, a towel wrapped around her. I later learnt she thought she was having a nightmare and thought it would wake her up. I offered to help dress her, but she quietly declined. I felt lost and scared, I didn't know what to do with myself, I had never been in a situation like this before. But, me being me I put my let's get things done head on, so I started to do the washing. As I was sorting through the basket, Kai's clothes that he had worn to school the day before were at the bottom, I couldn't wash them. They smelt of him, and I knew that would be the last time I would ever smell him again. My heart broke all over again.

Terri and Lily-Rose arrived, the police had picked them up, why I hadn't thought to go and get them I still don't know to this day. Terri looked worried but calm, Lily-Rose was completely heart broken, I held her so tight but, again, I didn't have the right words to make it better, I could only try and reassure her. Later that morning the doctor arrived to see Vikki, who was lying on her bed, I took him up to see her. He tried talking to her, but she was completely zoned out (she did this a lot in the later weeks and months). She wouldn't even look or acknowledge him. I explained what had happened and how Vikki had been talking of killing herself, he decided to give her a prescription of diazepam to help her rest.

Later that day Vikki came back downstairs, family and friends were arriving to comfort her and pay their respects. Vikki asked me to make phone calls to everyone. They were the hardest calls I had ever had to make, over and over the disbelief, the shock, the crying and the silence was just awful. The change in voices is something that lives with me. Because of the way Kai had passed a policeman had to be present, he was a lovely young man. I tried very hard to make him feel as comfortable as possible, he felt as if he was intruding and really didn't want to be there, but he had a job to do. Kai's bedroom had to be treated as a crime scene, I hated it, but I understood why. The forensic team came, and they took photos of everything and asked lots of questions. When they left they took with them some of Kai's possessions in brown paper bags, I hated that. It made me feel so angry, I wanted to stop them taking it all, but I knew I couldn't, they had a job to do.

My recollection of the rest of that day is very hazy, I remember Scott and Vikki going to see Kai in hospital, and thinking I need to take the children home with me. I didn't want them to see their mum and their dad so incredibly upset. Terri organised their clothes and pjs while I went to tell them what was happening. I hated leaving Vikki's house because I knew the next time I went back the house would never be the same again. I phoned Steve on the way home, which was so hard. I asked him to explain to Jude what had happened as I knew Jude would be excited to see the children but would have no understanding of why they were so upset.

The next day I remember feeling so upset, I didn't stop crying that day. Our boy's birthdays. The anger kicked in and I hated the world, why Kai? Why now? Why the day before his 16th birthday? Nothing made sense and it still doesn't. How could I look at Jude and wish him happy birthday? How could I face the world again? The 20th January 2018 is the worst day I had ever experienced in my life, life will never be the same again. I have learnt that it is ok, not to be ok.

***

A note from Lily-Rose

8:28 am, Saturday the 20th of January 2018 is a time and date that will forever and will be engraved in my mind as the darkest and worst day of my life. It was a gloomy morning weather wise and I woke up to the sound of my mum shouting on the phone, that's when I checked the time and it was so early. What the hell is wrong at this time of day was my first thought. In fact, I thought that someone was being attacked on the other side of the call as I could hear the fear in my mum's voice, while trying to calm down and reassure the other person on the other side of the call and also sounding frantic at the same time repeating the words, "Who's dead?". As I asked her what was wrong, what had happened and who she was speaking to, she looked me in the eye with a look of panic and said, "It's Vikki, she's screaming and crying he's dead, but I don't know who or what she's on about". My mum rang her back immediately as she couldn't understand her, or the name she was saying, so she hung up the phone to ring back, hoping for her voice to be a bit clearer. My first thought was that my brother-in-law, Scott, had been rushed to hospital, because he had been ill recently and there was no one else she could be on about, or so I thought. Scott answered straight away and that's when my mum realised, it was Kai, the boy who managed to fight through everything put against him was suddenly gone without a warning sign. The boy who not even a week before was jumping on me, pulling me into endless hugs and trying to annoy me by kicking, jumping and dribbling on me to try and wind me up.

Strangely enough it took me a few seconds to realise what she had said, and then it came. The disbelief, anger and sadness. All at once in a huge wave that I wasn't strong enough to handle. My legs went weak and I fell to the ground screaming at what I had just heard, as I was certain what I had just been told wasn't true or I was having a nightmare. Pinching myself, I asked why, why it was always Kai. Why, in a world so bad would a boy so good get taken away, especially the day before his 16th birthday, which Vikki and I had been discussing so much and dreading him turning this old so much the year before and particularly that month. Why was he continuously hurt or put through so much? Why would my sister, brother-in-law, nieces and nephew go through this immense pain of losing someone they loved with all their hearts when they did nothing to deserve this. I pulled myself up and glanced over at my mum, she has always been the strong one in our family, and that's when I realised, she was just as hurt as me and that this is her grandson and always will be, so I had to at least try to be a quarter of how strong she is and walked over and gave her a hug.

Mum and I were getting ready to go to Vikki and Scott's house as we knew they needed love and reassurance right now. Over the last few years of moving closer to my sister and her family, we had become much closer. I had been there every school holiday, almost every weekend and slept there whenever I missed them continuously for so long, and now all of them times would never be the same. As soon as I got into the police car, it felt like a slap in the face, a slap in the face from reality as it had now all become so much more real and I couldn't deny it anymore. The policemen were lovely from what I heard when they said hello, but I blocked the

93

rest of that car journey out and just sat there, so it's very vague.

Stepping out of the car was even more of a challenge. As I looked up, my face swollen from crying and drenched in tears, I could see Honey-Mae and Daisy waving and smiling at me through Julie and Alan's window. It wasn't about me being heartbroken anymore, I had to be strong for them, so I wiped my tears and waved and smiled back and walked into the home which now felt like a place so unfamiliar, even though I spent most of my life here. We went through the back door and awaiting us was Beckie. Mum went straight upstairs to see Vikki, as she had just got out the shower, as I walked over to the sofa and sat staring at a picture of Kai's beautiful face. Beckie came over and sat with me, giving me a hug, which was so tight I remember praying I would wake up from this nightmare as I came out of it. That wasn't the last of all those hugs that day as so many people were in and out of the house. I then went upstairs because I knew my sister was now at the lowest she would ever be, and I had to try to be there for her. As soon as I went in, I could hear her screaming and howling. I sat beside her and she was shaking so much I had to help her hold her drink someone had put into her hand. Nothing I would have said in that moment would have helped, mainly because she was zoned out and wasn't listening, and secondly because what can you say to a mother who had spent basically 16 years caring for a boy she loved so deeply and would do anything for to try and heal that pain, not one single thing.

I came back down stairs and knew my niece and nephew, who were only next door, needed me. So, I went around, faking a smile harder than I ever have before and was bombarded by hugs from the girls. There is one thing that plays through my head, along with many others from that day, which is Daisy, she ran up to me smiling and looked me straight in the eye and said," Lily-rose, I hope Kai is okay, can we go and see him at the hospital?" I didn't know what to say and I knew I wasn't the one who should tell her what had happened, so I just smiled at her, trying to not give her too much hope. I gave them all a kiss on the head but Bailey, as I knew he would really hate that, and then told them I loved them all. I was in and out that day taking toys and clothes back and forth trying to keep their minds off what they had seen. Vikki and Scott later came around and broke the news to children, I was sitting with them when they did, it's the hardest thing I have ever had to watch.

That night I hardly slept; I got to sleep around 3:45am and then was woken up at 4:00am as I could hear Vikki walking around in the kitchen with Mum, crying. It was Kai's birthday and for a split second, the thing I had been non-stop crying about over the last 24 hours was forgotten about and I thought it wasn't real. This was my first experience of death, that I can truly remember, of someone I was so close to and loved with all my heart. Kai wasn't just a nephew he was more like a brother, he was older than me and wouldn't let me forget about it. He always tried to prove he was taller and would attempt to squash me if I proved him wrong as I am much taller than him.

Before the 20th of January, in my whole 14 years of life, I had only ever seen my big sister cry twice before this, and I knew that this wouldn't be the last and I would see it many more times as a piece of her heart was taken with Kai and will forever be with him, the same goes for Scott. Even though he comes across as tough man who is so strong and full of jokes, he is hurting too, a piece of his heart was also taken with Kai's and I will forever admire them both for continuing to be so strong for each other and their kids and being the best parents Kai could ever have had. If there is one thing that I have taken away from Kai's passing, it is to remind those who you love that you love them because you never know when the last time you will be able to tell them.

***

I remember Corina in the corner crying, she had come to help with the kids and to check on Scott and me. I remember Dot and Rose making everyone tea while I sat on the sofa with no idea how I got there. I felt like time had stood still while people whizzed around me, ambulance men and police in and out. Scott holding my hand one minute and gone the next, I could hear voices, but I couldn't make out what was being said. Beckie trying to stay strong for everyone. I remember crying one minute for my brother, Thomas, and then he was next to me. My phone kept pinging and ringing which irritated me but snapped me back into focus. I picked my phone up and saw that neighbours had text me, as well as Joanie who used to look after Kai at nursery. All with the same question, 'Is everything ok? Is Kai ok?' I realised that time had passed, and I hadn't told anyone, my family and friends and Kai's school they all needed to know. I don't remember writing it, but I remember thinking the best way to let everyone know was to write it on Facebook. I wrote, 'My beautiful boy gained his angel wings this morning, we are heartbroken.' I turned my phone off and curled into a ball screaming again.

The ambulance men took my baby away from his home for the last time, I don't remember it. Scott went to the hospital with the police and I know how hard that must have been as he didn't want to leave me. I sat in shock, completely numb, with the police still around, and I remember sitting and thinking this isn't real. I was dreaming, this was all a bad dream, I just needed to wake up. I walked into the shower and stood under the running water waiting for the cold to wake me from the nightmare I was having. When that didn't work I got out walked upstairs and threw some clothes on, maybe if I went back to my bed I would wake up. More people were arriving by the minute, Terri and Lily-Rose, my dad, Tom, my brother, Jamie, and my sisters, Katie and Georgia. I don't remember a single thing, just the immense guilt I had caused to everyone. Looking at their tear stained faces and knowing I was the reason their hearts had broken. The doctor came out as everyone was alarmed and worried about me, I was screaming I wanted to kill myself and I wanted to be with my boy. I don't remember the doctor arriving, I didn't even acknowledge him the state I was in. Beckie dealt with it all as I lay trying to block it all out and convince myself I had been in an accident. I was in a coma and would wake up and this would all have been a bad dream.

I remember speaking to Adele and 'Little Mum', Jodie, I cannot recall anything that was said, one minute I was on the phone the next Adele was at my side.

***

A note from Adele

20th January, just a normal rainy-day weekend. I sat in bed with a cup of tea talking to my children about what we could do. My phone rings, it flashed up with Vikki's name, nothing unusual so I answer. "He is dead." The world stopped as I tried to understand what Vik was saying. He is dead? Who is dead? I check my phone to double check that I am talking to Vik and the panic sets in. I still have no idea who she is talking about and what is going on. "What? Who is dead Vik? What is going on?" I ramble as I hear sobbing on the other end of the line. "Kai," she whispered, and my heart broke into a thousand pieces. No, this isn't right, he isn't dead I think to myself, all I could offer Vik was a crying, "No." My mind kicks in, where is she? She needs you! I ask, "Where are you, Vik?" and she replied, "I don't know." I knew I had to be with her, "I'm coming over." I don't care if I have to stand outside in the rain, Vik needs me.

98

Fifteen minutes later, I am stood at the top of my best friends drive. The police car parked outside tells me something is going on, but I still can't believe Kai is dead. I gather my courage to walk to the house and knock on the door. What the hell am I going to say? Is all that I am thinking. I knock, and Beckie answers, the grief on her face tells me it is true. I burst into tears and Beckie gives me the biggest cuddle. This beautiful woman has had her heart ripped out, but here she is giving me courage. Beckie is an amazing woman, a living angel.

She takes me into the living room and tells me what happened, I sit quietly as I try to take in the horror of the fact that Kai has gone. It's not right, he was dancing around the living room the night before and singing. Vikki had sent me the video on what's app, how can he be gone forever? Beckie takes my hand and leads me upstairs. I am stealing strength from Beckie to find the courage to be strong for Vik, she needs everyone right now. I was not prepared for what I saw, to be honest I had no clue what to expect from a mother who had just lost her child. Vik was sat on her bed holding Scott's hand, but it wasn't my Vik. She looked so fragile and distant, the twinkle in her eyes was gone, she sat staring. She didn't hear us come in, Beckie told her I was here and then her eyes met mine. She said two words, "I'm sorry." I couldn't stop the tears from falling, they were so violent my whole body shook. I climbed onto the bed and took her hand, desperate for anything to say to make it better, but knowing nothing ever would. "I am so sorry Vik," I cried. I felt Vik shake with emotion and she threw her head back and screamed. That sound

99

will haunt me for the rest of my life, that sound was a heart breaking and a soul screaming in pain. I scrambled to hold Vik and to stop the sound because it broke my heart.

I stayed most of the day at Vik's, she doesn't remember as she retreated into the back of her mind, a bodies safety reaction to a trauma your mind knows will break you if it doesn't keep you safe. I hugged people I knew and people I didn't that day, because that's the beauty of the Hammonds, they are an amazing family. People came and went to show their love and support. Scott truly blew me away that day, he was on auto-pilot, but he was talking and trying to make sense of it all. He made the tea and the food and sat with the love of his life trying to put her back together. I will never forget the day Kai died, the world is a darker place without him in it. But, I will always remember the love that is ever present in the Hammond house, love for each other and friends, and ultimately Kai. I miss you so much, Kai.

***

Scott came home from the hospital, he later told me that he was put onto a ward with a thin curtain separating the bays, and they put Kai in the next bay to him. I was fuming when I found this out, Scott's brothers, Brett and Clint, were with him and supported him as he answered questions, signed consent forms and requested a post mortem. How Scott managed to do all that after all we had been through that morning I will never know. We had swapped roles that day, and Scott was now the strong one.

I was back on the sofa with no idea how I had got there, the police Family Liaison Officer wanted to question me, along with two other ladies, as with any sudden death of a child under 16 it I always treated as suspicious. The only part I remember is one of the ladies asking if it was correct that I was a mother of four. This sent me into a rage and I cried my eyes out shouting, "I am a mum of five!" Scott and Beckie stayed in the room to calm me and to help, as right now I wasn't making any sense at all. Beckie, I now know, wanted them to question me later as she felt I was in no fit state, but they insisted. Ria arrived, and I don't recall anything as a whole room full of people sat in silence, no one had any words, nothing would make this better.

***

A note from Ria

"I must pull over at the shop for..." I thought to myself as I shifted the car swiftly to the side of the road and glanced down at my phone. A message from my son's relative lit up the phone screen. "Curious," I thought. I pulled on the handbrake and slid my thumb over the screen to open the message, a message that would change everything. "*Is Kai ok?*" The message read. What did she mean? I replied in confusion questioning her message. Her response deafened me although only through a text. My heart began to thump, and the colour drained from my face. I knew this feeling only too well, but surely this was a false alarm - A misunderstanding.

You can't trust everything you read on social media, I comforted myself. I rang my Auntie Wendy, I knew she would know what to do. She would call Auntie Beckie and settle it as nothing more than a mix-up. I sat and waited for the call back, still in the car at the side of the road. I slid my thumb across the screen again and placed the phone to my ear. My fears were met with sobs, Wendy's apologies for the bad news she had to deliver to me. The worst news. The worst possible news, Kai had gone. A yelp of pain exited my body at that point, one I had no control over, followed closely by a barrage of tears. "No," I thought to myself, my mind flooded with images of Vikki and Scott, like a cinematic flashback of all the years I had watched them devote everything to him. Kai, my very dearest friend.

The thing is with situations like this, you can never plan for it, prepare for it, or know how you are going to deal or cope with it. It's at this point you almost enter a twilight zone. Where reality disappears, and shock takes over. This is how I found Vikki that day.

On arriving outside that well-kept little home, I had visited so many times, in the road I knew so well, I was greeted with an atmosphere that was alien to the warmth and love that usually lingered in the air of that quiet country lane. There was a police presence. Apologies could be heard, confessing they were just doing their job. Huddled together for support in the beautifully decorated kitchen, family and friends all equally devastated for the Hammonds and, also, for themselves, because that was the thing about Kai, if you knew him, he made a mark. An everlasting mark in your heart, a connection that words couldn't always explain. Auntie Beckie hugged me close. I felt her tremble uncontrollably and she began to cry, though I could tell they were not her first tears of the day. She explained what had happened and that I would have to wait until the police had left to see Vikki and Scott. I nodded, as affectionately as I knew how, to the congregation in the kitchen. Vikki and I had always joked about how awful we both were at showing our emotions or letting them out. This was one of the first moments in my life when I wasn't sure I had control of mine.

I sat silently at the kitchen table next to Adele, we smiled at one another sharing glimpses of the pain we had for our dear friends. Minutes seemed to stretch further than the longest hour, all concept of time lost in the well of grief that consumed the room. I glanced many times at Vikki's youngest sister, Lily-Rose, visualising her as the little girl I remembered running around in the sunshine in Vikki and Scott's garden years ago. Now, she was overwhelmed with the pain of losing someone she loved so very much.

After a while, Adele and I went outside to the garage for some fresh air. It was the first time I really spoke. I stumbled over my words because they had no real purpose, what could words do? They are my friends and I can't help them fix this. Auntie Beckie came in to say Vikki could see me, be brave I told myself, whatever that means. Approaching the living room, I saw Scott, I hugged him and kissed his cheek.

103

Slowly, I entered the front room, I looked around, but my friend wasn't there. There was no laughter, no warmth, all the things I knew of her, of them, was gone. It felt like Kai had left and he had taken them with him. Vikki was sat motionless on the small sofa at the side of the room. Her gaze at the wall was undisturbed by any movement in the room. I sat beside her, scared to touch her for fear that she might disappear altogether. I placed a hand on her leg and searched the emptiness in my head for something that would ease her suffering that would soothe her pain. Suddenly, she turned and looked at me. "Ria, what do I do?" she said. All I could offer was, "I don't know." We hugged. I have never held anyone so tight. Vikki cried a cry that will stay with me forever.

As I looked around I realised I didn't know, Vikki didn't know, Scott didn't know, Auntie Beckie didn't know. No one knew what to do. I mean what are you supposed to do if you wake one morning and the sun isn't in the sky? Even through the clouds Kai would warm your day. He could bring light to your darkest moment, your saddest thought. He was the rarest sort of person that made life worth living. That made you appreciate the small things like, the smell of fresh cooked chip-shop chips, the feeling of water rippling over your skin, the laughter that makes you hold your tummy and roll over. Kai was, and will forever be, the most beautiful person the world has ever known. When I left that day, everything had changed.

***

I needed to see my babies who were still next door. I walked around, I don't remember who was with me or how I made it. I stepped into the already open door to be met by Julie and Alan. Julie hugged me so tight and I could feel she wanted to take the pain away. I don't recall anything I said at all, I walked in to see Bailey and Honey-Mae, and they looked at me half hoping, half knowing. "Is Kai ok, Mum?" Bailey asked. I remember breaking it to them both as Honey-Mae stood shell shocked, and Bailey sobbed in my arms. Lola didn't understand and was cuddling my legs happy to see me. I walked through the kitchen and Daisy saw me, she ran to the sofa curled into a ball and screamed "No, no, no," over, and over again. She put her fingers in her ears and just kept wailing and sobbing. I had never heard my child make such a sound and it stunned me into silence. I sat beside her and pulled her onto my lap, I cradled her as I made her look into my eyes. "I am so sorry, Daisy," I said, and with that she screamed and howled and threw her body back, trying to get rid of the pain inside of her. I didn't need to say anymore, she knew her best friend had gone.

I had an overwhelming urge to be with Kai, I wasn't waking from this nightmare no matter how much I tried. My mind was a fog of panic and denial, he couldn't be dead, not Kai. I must have dreamt everything, but I knew the longer the day went on and the more that was happening, dreams didn't have this much detail. So, I shut it out, curled into a ball, only making a sound to scream, only moving to attack myself. I suddenly had an overwhelming urge to be with Kai. If I could see him, if he could see me and see how distressed I was, he would wake up. I was determined that he would sit up for his mum and pull me into his head lock hug and snuggle into my hair like he always did. I remember telling Beckie and Scott I needed to see Kai and I needed to see him now. Beckie made all the arrangements with Stacey, my beautiful friend, who worked at the hospital. The next minute, I was being driven to the hospital with my brother Thomas, and Scott. I don't remember saying a single word, each step felt a huge effort when we got out of the car. People were sitting around drinking coffee and walking about their business, and I wanted to scream at them all. How could they be carrying on? Why was everything around me the same yet my life had changed in an instant.

Walking in to see Kai was like someone had stepped inside my body, it didn't feel like it was my own. I felt weaker than I had ever felt, tired and drained, everything felt like it didn't belong to me and my footsteps felt alien. I walked into the room and saw Kai laying on the bed, covers pulled over his body, his little hand that I used to hold was clutching a teddy. I looked at his face hoping and praying this was a mistake, it had happened before, people were supposed to have died and then woken up. Kai didn't look like Kai, his lips were parted, his tongue now not visible, his eyes were tightly closed and his nose that I lovingly stroked every day was swollen. His colour wasn't blue anymore but there was no mistaking that that was my baby laying there. An overwhelming urge to touch him came over me, but I resisted, I knew that if I did, I would not let go of him. I backed into a corner and the guilt came rushing through me, you did this, this is your fault, you gave him a pillow, you slept through the night when he needed you. You killed him. I couldn't stop of the thoughts as I began sobbing hysterically, leaning against the wall to support me. "I'm so sorry Kai, I love you so very much and I am so sorry," was all I could say before we left.

The day dragged on, Beckie collected some of the children's things to take them back home with her. Terri and Lily-Rose, both still in their own grief and shock, stayed with us that night and didn't leave for weeks. I sat in stunned silence as the first sprinkle of snow came, "It snowed the day he came home," I said to Scott. I don't remember the rest of the day, I climbed into bed exhausted and pulled the quilt over me. I lay sobbing with the light on, Scott came in and put his arms around me as we both lay sobbing together. Every time I closed my eyes I pictured Kai's face, blue and still. Scott turned the light out and I began screaming for it to be left on, I didn't want to see Kai like that. I didn't sleep at all and just lay all night staring at the wall. Thinking over, and over again, what am I going to do?

21st JANUARY

I came downstairs for a bath at 4.00am, I don't know why but laying still was driving me insane. I sat in the bath curled into a ball sobbing until I made myself heave. I went upstairs to get dressed then went back downstairs to find Terri still awake. We sat at the kitchen table, both in silence and I realised what day it was. Kai's 16th birthday. I started to scream again, hitting myself and shouting. I was full of rage, mainly at myself. Terri took me in her arms as Scott came up behind me and cuddled me.

    The snow came thick and fast, I sat in a daze not knowing what to do. I knew I couldn't take this pain inside of me anymore, I couldn't live without Kai. He was my best friend, my light and my reason for having strength. I decided I wanted to go for a walk, I would walk as far away as I could to the railway track in a field I knew. I was going to end this misery, I couldn't live with the guilt of my baby's death on my shoulders, no one needed me here now.

What use was I to anyone in this state? I would never be the same person again, Scott would hate me when he woke up and realised that this was my fault. Everyone was being nice now, but when they truly thought about it they would know it was my fault. I just wanted to walk as far as I could, in the snow, and slip away to end this pain for me and for everyone. I started to pull on my shoes and coat, and Terri asked where I was going, I told her I just needed to be on my own as I felt smothered and I needed to think. "I will come with you," she said. "No, I want to be alone." I could see Terri thinking and then the relief on her face when Scott came in. "You aren't being alone Vikki, wait for me I will come with you." I cried and pleaded I just wanted to be alone, but Scott wouldn't have it. He pulled his shoes and coat on and we walked together in the snow, no words were said, He knew. He saved my life that day.

Coming home, I walked into Kai's room full of his 16th birthday presents, it hit me like a punch to the gut, he would never see them, he wouldn't get to eat the cake I had ordered or go for the meal we had planned. Beckie had cancelled the cake for me, and later Jemma, The Cakey Lady, didn't charge me for the cake, she sent it into Kai's school for his friends to enjoy, which really touched me. I never have thanked her properly for doing such a lovely thing for us. There were so many visits and phone calls, I don't remember who came and who phoned. I sat in a world of my own, trying to climb into the wall of silence I had created that didn't hurt so bad in there. Reality was now cold and raw, every time I snapped out of my zone I would be howling and screaming all over again as the pain crashed over me in huge waves.

Alan and Julie came around, and I couldn't even look at Alan as guilt ate away at me, I had caused this man to see the worst possible image of my son. I had selfishly wanted him to take away my pain and fix it like he had before. He now looked haunted, haunted by the very images even I, myself, couldn't cope with. Every time I closed my eyes, or if the light was out I would start screaming again, as I couldn't cope with seeing my Kai like that in my mind's eye. I am forever thankful to Alan and Julie, who I later found out, had an open house for my friends and family the day Kai left us, being comforted and looked after when it all got too much seeing me next door.

Scott's brothers and my Dad Darren, also came, as did my brother, Charlie, and a long-term family friend, Danny. I don't remember much of that day at all. I spent it laying curled up wishing I could rewind time. I couldn't even look at Scott, the guilt I felt was crushing me. I had ripped this family apart, I hadn't been there for my son. Now, my kids and husband would have the very image in their minds that I couldn't cope with. I remember sobbing to Scott to leave me, I didn't deserve him, he would only blame me in the coming weeks and months and I couldn't blame him one bit. He should leave me now, I had killed his son how could he stand to even look at me? Scott sobbed cuddling me, and told me no one was to blame, Kai had died suddenly, no one knew why, but it most certainly wasn't anyone's fault. We didn't hear him, he looked as if he was sleeping. He

110

wasn't going anywhere if I liked it or not, and to this day that man has never left my side.

Stacey was in constant contact with me throughout and still to this day, as she worked at the hospital she kept me fully informed with permission of her boss. She arranged for us to be able to take Kai his birthday presents, the present I had lovingly wrapped. I sat outside the room with Hannah, my sister-in- law, as Scott and Clint went in to see Kai and hand some clean clothes and presents to the staff. I couldn't face seeing Kai, not today, the guilt was all consuming.

SILENCE

The house was so silent, our house was never silent, Kai would be humming through the kid's TV shows, climbing and jumping on your lap for a cuddle, there was never a quiet moment. Now, I could hear the birds singing, the flurry of snow bouncing off my windows, and cars driving past. It made me angry, I hadn't noticed those sounds before and I didn't want to notice them now. I was in contact with the FLO who kept me up to date with what was happening. Kai was having a post mortem as we requested, I couldn't imagine not knowing why this had happened. I needed to know why, as did Scott.

Kai's teacher messaged me - we then had a long chat on the phone, both crying and trying to find out how a child so full of life on Friday was now not here. Amy was a huge source of comfort in the following weeks, checking in on me and phoning, even through her own grief, going back to school after the shock of the weekend must have been so hard on her but she still found time to comfort me. Kai's school were all in a state of shock. I received many messages of support from teachers, parents, and helpers, that I still haven't read them all to this day as they hurt so much. I know one day I will find so much comfort from their kind words.

The kids were finding it so difficult to function, they were home, trying to get used to the silence in their once lively house. Their schools were amazing and supportive and to this day continue to be. Counselling was arranged for all of them through the school. I had no energy to even communicate with them, Corina was doing the school runs for me. As was Scott and Terri after a few weeks. I would lay in bed and pretend that Kai had gone to school, then I would get up and sit in silence on the sofa and disappear back to bed when they got in from school. I couldn't handle Kai not being there when they all came home. For the next few months my children lost their mum, Scott lost his wife and my friends lost their friend. I wasn't myself in anyway, I couldn't concentrate. I wasn't sleeping at all and refused to take the diazepam the doctor had prescribed. I convinced myself that this pain I was feeling was deserved. I should feel every single part of it because it was my fault. I only ate when forced and lost over a stone and a half in a matter of weeks. Scott couldn't go back to work as he couldn't leave me, and Terri and Lily-Rose stayed for weeks helping. I got up when the kids were all sorted, laying there pretending Kai was now at school, and spent the days staring at the walls. People were in and out the whole time, some days I would acknowledge them, other days

113

they wouldn't even get a hello from me. Cards, gifts and flowers arrived by the hundreds, I had never seen so many gifts in my life. Paula and Nick, who have a son with TSC, had always been a huge support to me, their daughter, Jess, set up a charity just before Kai had passed away. It is called William's Wishes and the aim is to give many families something to smile about. Their first donation was a huge box addressed to us; the children each received sweets and a beautiful build a bear teddy. With it came a framed picture of Kai with a beautiful poem. I will never forget what that meant to us, and often think what an amazing family they are, going through their own battles and still having time to make others smile.

We had nothing but miscommunication from the FLO over the following weeks. I was told there was a hold up with the post mortem as they couldn't decide how best to proceed. Kai was one day short of his 16th birthday which would have made him an adult, yet he was still a child. There was debates whether he should have been treated as a child or as an adult. This would then determine which hospital Kai would have his post mortem at. Our local one, which he was at, or GOSH. This sent me into a panic, Kai had never been to GOSH on his own and I didn't want him there alone now. Every time I thought of him lying there it made me feel sick to my stomach. He was all alone, as he was when he died, which I will never forgive myself for. Eventually, it was agreed that Kai could have his post mortem at our local hospital. We had so many big decisions to make that my head was spinning. Everyone we needed for this to be done as quickly as possible was on holiday or going on holiday. I felt rage bubble up inside of me. Why was there no hurry? How had they left me with four other children who were now back at home and not hurry this along? I phoned the FLO screaming at her down the phone that if this was one of my other children would this have been more of a priority? Did they just accept Kai had died because he was disabled? They didn't know Kai, he fought everything possible. How could he simply go to bed singing and not wake up? None of it made sense and the lack of urgency was driving me insane. I couldn't understand how they were so quick to assume how Kai had died when I was confused as ever. I spent hours on the internet researching how Kai could have died when I stumbled across SUDEP. Sudden Unexplained Death in Epilepsy. As I read other people's stories, it made my stomach turn. They were nearly always found in bed, having passed away in the night. No symptoms and no warning signs. One person had been talking on facetime to a loved one and they simply stopped talking and died. One lady was chatting to her daughter in another room only to be met with silence. Hundreds of people had woken up having heard nothing or seeing nothing, to find their loved one dead, even with the use of monitors to detect seizures. As I read on I knew this had to be the most likely cause of how Kai died.

Kai's consultant, Dr James, rang to express his sympathies. He was so lovely and told me we were his favourite family, and that he admired how much love there was between us all. He gave me such comforting words and brought up the word SUDEP. Kai's doctor later phoned and again gave me a lovely message, he also said SUDEP to me. I started to look into it more, joining a group on Facebook and asking lots of questions. I was alarmed to find that just like me no one else had known the risks of SUDEP before their loved one died. I decided to phone the SUDEP support line and spent many hours on the phone to a lovely lady, who listened to my cries, my rage, and my guilt. She answered every question I had and talked me through what would happen next. SUDEP Action were a huge support to me over the coming weeks and I can never thank them enough for taking the time to listen to me. They told me that even with a paramedic on the scene nothing would have prevented Kai's death at all. Even if I was asleep next to him I wouldn't have known as it would have been silent and quick. Kai wouldn't have felt any pain at all, he would have gone to sleep and never woke up, not having a clue. I started to put all the pieces together and realised Kai couldn't possibly have had a seizure and suffocated. I had spent so long reading about how painful suffocation was and torturing myself that he struggled and hearing this brought me comfort to think he wouldn't have known. Kai was in his cosy position knees to his chin on his front, if he'd had a seizure he would have been flat out and unable to get back into his cosy position. I thought back to when I lifted him up to give him CPR, he was dry, I was sure of it. If he'd had a seizure, he would have soaked through his clothes and bedding. I phoned the police to beg them to check Kai's bedding and clothes, and they were dry. I would have also have heard it, instead I heard nothing at all. I knew in my heart Kai didn't have a seizure and suffocate, but my head kept torturing me, what if he suffocated and the whole time he struggled I was asleep?

The first week after Kai died I refused to take my medication the doctor had prescribed, and I was driving myself insane, I gave in and started to take a high dose of diazepam. They numbed me and made me sleep the whole night through. I just needed to not feel, not think, and not be me for a while and they helped me over the following few weeks. Donna, my beautiful psychic friend, was in touch and phoned to give me a reading from Kai. I answered the phone and we spent the first few minutes just crying down the phone. Donna gave me such a beautiful spot on personal message, I don't think she realises to this day how much it helped me. She told me Kai had died suddenly, he didn't feel a thing, and that my mum, Nan and Scott's grandparents were waiting to take him. He knew I wanted to be with him, to end it all and he told me we would be together soon, but not now. It wasn't my time and he didn't need me yet, my kids did. She also told me that Scott would be doing a huge garden project, she could see wood and lots of digging. She said Kai would be in his blue hoody I had chosen, but he wanted to be in his green one, and he would get his way. At the time this meant nothing to me, how could we be thinking of a project when we had just lost our son? Later, her words came back to me and I couldn't believe how spot on she would be. She started to cry again and told me she'd had a dream about Kai two weeks before he died, she woke up sweating and woke her husband for comfort. She had dreamt that Kai had died, she didn't think it was a vision at the time, as she was asleep. It was so clear it really upset her, her husband comforted her and told her it was just a dream. How ironic we had both dreamt a very similar dream two weeks before my baby passed away. Donna agreed that it was a way of letting us know, to try to prepare us, but we both brushed it aside, this was Kai after all, he got through anything thrown at him. Donna continued to be a tower of strength to Scott and me over the following weeks and months, and still to this day.

I was finding it hard to put one foot in front of the other, I was drugged up on diazepam and spent most of my days in a complete bubble. I fell asleep on the sofa after having so many days of not sleeping and woke a little while later. I looked across to Kai's seat and saw Lily-Rose sitting there, and for a minute I thought it was Kai. My vision snapped into focus and I realised it wasn't, that feeling of reality hit me and I began to scream, Terri and Lily-Rose both held me as I sobbed my heart out. I never ever fell asleep during the day again. I found it hard trying to come to terms with what had happened and was still in a state of shock, I won't go into how my children dealt with it as it is their personal journey and I don't feel its right to share. Some things I've held back, but as you can imagine it was tough. At different ages they struggled immensely, how they went back to school a week after, I am in awe of them all. They were all terrified of Kai's room now, every time one of them went past to the kitchen they would shake or scream and cry. Kai's room was a no-go area, and it made me feel sad that the heart of the home now held such horrendous images in our minds. Kai's equipment had to go back and his bed we were so excited about needed to go back to the charity. I stayed upstairs when they came, Terri and Scott dealt with them. His wheelchair went back to the wheelchair services, and his wheelchair a lovely family from Essex gave to us went to a charity so someone else could get use from it. All that was left was Kai's bubble tube, sensory lights, toys, and his clothes. I phoned Stacey and decided to donate his sensory lights to the local hospital, I didn't want it sat at home having no use. Kai had so much love for those lights and I knew the hospital were crying out for sensory equipment. So, we took them to Stacey and Kelly, who we sat with talking for ages, and they promised us they would be well loved and appreciated. We later got a picture of Kai's corner in the hospital, as much as it made me cry, I knew we had done the right thing.

Stacey handed us a wooden box, inside were Kai's footprints and strands of his hair, they couldn't get a hand print from him as his little fists were still gripped shut. Stacey told us all about a lady who made necklaces from hand prints and Scott later ordered me a necklace of Kai's toe print that I wear every day. Sitting in Kai's empty room for the first time was horrendous, I felt angry that his room was empty, it hit me like a punch to the stomach that this was real, Kai wasn't coming back, ever. I remember raging and throwing things around before falling on the floor and howling until I couldn't cry anymore. I wanted to sleep in Kai's room to feel closer to him, and we decided to move our bed into Kai's room. We now have his room and made it ours and it was the best thing we could have done. Scott did most of it himself, and Adele came over and helped us with the smaller things that needed doing. The children would now go in there, they sit and go through all of Kai's memory boxes and trunks, they watch TV in there, and they sit in his throne, something none of us would do before. That room door stayed closed for such a long time it made me so sad, I am so happy we now all felt closer to Kai in this way.

Every night we stood hand in hand, Scott, Bailey, Honey-Mae, Daisy, Lola and me watching the stars while playing Kai's favourite music. Four friends named star's after Kai, which was such a lovely gesture and meant the children had one each.

So much was happening during the first two weeks, I knew Kai's funeral needed preparing and we were told to make an appointment, which we did. It snowed every single day since Kai left us, it felt as if the weather was outraged as much as we were. Terri, Scott and Beckie were doing everything for me, shopping, cooking, ironing, feeding the kids, taking them to school, homework. I wasn't their mum for a good few months in the early stages, I had no energy to be, I was there, but I may as well have not been. I cannot thank Scott, who was going through his own grief and torment, enough for keeping me standing over those dark months. Suicide was often in my thoughts; how easy it would be to end this pain my mind would say. Take those tablets and this hell will be over, I battled every single day and still sometimes do. I made a pros and cons list of why I shouldn't be here, the guilt was eating me up inside, the not knowing if I could have saved my boy. I begged Scott on so many occasions to let me die, I would howl and rage in his arms that an animal suffering would be put out of its misery, how was I expected to live like this? I screamed at him that he was selfish to expect me to stay, I reminded him daily I was only here for him and the kids and how much I resented them for making me stay. The man put up with all of it, my sobbing as he sat listening to me pleading with him to let me go, holding me when I got angry and stroking me when the tears dried up and my body involuntary jolted with pain. Never once did he blame me, say an angry word, shout or scream, he took it all. He knew I blamed myself and couldn't make me stop. He tried, he pleaded, he bargained, he stated facts, but I wouldn't listen. I told him time and time again he couldn't love a murderer, leave, go, he would eventually anyway when the results came back his son suffocated while I happily slept through it. Everyone was being nice to me now, but they must have been judging me - How can a mother sleep while her son lay dying, how did she not know?

Scott went through his own hell, and we both became paranoid that people were watching our every move. I wouldn't leave the house unless Scott was by my side and only to an appointment about Kai, or to a meeting at one of the kid's schools. I would hide and look around to make sure no one I knew was about. I felt like everyone, even people who didn't know me, was staring at me. We shut the blinds early every night, in case someone went past and looked in, imaging what they would think if we were smiling at that point at something one of the kids had done. I had never been one to care about what anyone thinks, but still to this day I get paranoid people are judging. Every little thing became a big deal. Would people think we didn't care if we took the kids out or went for a meal. It played on my mind constantly and I felt like I deserved the judgement, yet no one ever judged us. Checking my emails, I read Kai had been accepted for an anti-suffocation pillow I had applied for, I felt sick. I read and re read the email over and over. If he'd had that pillow would it have saved his life? I only applied as I had that dream and the constant fear that Kai would die, I didn't for a second think he needed it. I had also applied for a seizure alarm, which again was accepted, and the email came through with the pillow email days after Kai had died. It felt like a sick joke, like God mocking me. If this was weeks earlier, he could have still been here. I phoned SUDEP and cried down the phone about the acceptance emails I had received, they listened and told me that there was no evidence at all to suggest that these would prevent SUDEP. Also, as I believed strongly Kai hadn't had a seizure in his death the monitor wouldn't have worked.

My friends were amazing, I was never alone. My house was constantly full of friends taking it in turns to sit with me. Some days I could talk and others I would sit in silence. Sarah, Amy, Corina, Stacey, Hailey, Adele and Jodie as well as Ria to name a few were constantly checking in on me. Little Mum, Jodie, was going through her own personal problems as she had been diagnosed with Lymphocyte-Rich Classic Hodgkin Lymphoma cancer. Yet she still found that little bit of energy she had left and reserved it all for me and my family in the coming weeks and months, and to this day. Our family were amazing, Scott's brothers rarely left his side, as did his aunt Sheila and my family were also around me when I needed them. Yet, with all these people I still felt more alone than I had ever felt in my life, I knew I would never feel a love as strong as I had with Kai.

The constant phoning and finding out why Kai's post mortem had been delayed was exhausting, I still convinced myself that he wasn't dead. They were hiding something from me, he was fine, and they wanted to keep him for himself. I tortured myself that he was looking for me, and he couldn't find me. Stacey kept in constant contact with me, she told me when they changed him into his clean tracksuit we got him for his birthday, his blue Puma hoody and bottoms, playing him his favourite Sam Smith songs. She told me they sat talking to him, telling him how loved he was and how much we missed him. She kept me going with her updates over those few weeks, reassuring me he wasn't alone. The FLO had some explaining to do, why was Kai's post mortem taking so long? She blamed everyone from the paramedics, to the police, to us, before admitting her own fuck up. The paramedics, she said, should have tried to resuscitate Kai, this infuriated me, he was very obviously dead when I found him. The police, she said, shouldn't have let anyone into our house as it was a crime scene at that point, this again infuriated me. The police that day were amazing, they made sure Kai's room was secure, not one person went in there until he was taken away by ambulance, and then of course the forensic team was there. Scott apparently didn't sign for a post mortem, this was a complete load of bollocks, Scott signed every form possible at the hospital with his brothers, consultants and the police as proof. She also tried to blame the nurses, saying that upon arrival they were very upset and got in the way of them doing their jobs. She told me that Kai was too stiff to get the required bloods and samples from, the word she used sent a bolt of pain through my heart. An insensitive term to use for someone's child who had passed away. She then dropped her own mistake, she hadn't done the paper work correctly, she had left out the most vital part, how I found Kai that morning! I was livid and from that day on I refused to have her in my home or answer her calls. She was more interested in where my carpet was from than the fact that I had just lost my son! I put a complaint in and got given a new FLO who was amazing. The less competent one's delays, her mistakes and her miscommunication delayed my sons post mortem and extended our pain further, and I don't care how bitter it makes me sound. I will never ever forgive her for that.

The appointment for Kai's funeral was surreal, I felt sick sitting there making plans for my son. I also hated the question asking how old he was. Because how old was he? Was he now 16? Or was he forever 15? Both answers stung. Scott and I sat squeezing each other's hand, biting on the inside of our cheeks to stop the tears falling. The funeral team were amazing, we said money wasn't a problem, we would find the money, we wanted Kai to have the very best of everything. We ordered doves to be released, white horses and carriage, funeral books, a condolence book. The funeral would take place at the local church that the kids went to with their school, we also asked for their reverend as we wanted to make it as less scary for them as we possibly could. We wanted Kai cremated, I couldn't stand the thought of him laying there in the ground, he hated the cold. I don't know how we got through that appointment, and we got home and sat exhausted for the rest of the day letting the reality kick in. Kai's school phoned and told us they were doing an assembly in celebration of Kai's life and we were invited to go. We were overwhelmed, and of course accepted the invitation.

Walking through Kai's school was so very hard, the tears fell as I looked around wishing I could hear him shout "Mum." I stumbled into the hall, cuddles were coming from everywhere, people were sitting crying and teachers were struggling to hold it together. The children could sense something was not right and the mood was sombre. Scott, Terri, Beckie and I all attended, we were overwhelmed to see so many people, some parents had turned up, old teachers that had now retired were also there. Kai's bus drivers, old and new, and friends, it took my breath away. I heard a rushing sound and turned around to see Kai's teacher, Amy, running towards me, arms outstretched, a look of pain etched all over her face as her tears fell. She ran into me and pulled me into the biggest hug as we both stood sobbing tightly holding onto one another to gain some strength. The assembly was beautiful, a student who couldn't make it even face timed in to listen and to watch. Tributes flashed up on screen, pictures of Kai's first day at school, to more recent ones of Kai swimming, dancing, covered in paint and food, dressed up, being massaged, image after image burst onto the screen as the head teacher, Dave, gave his speech.

Dave:

On Friday, I saw Kai walking through the school and I thought how well he looked. On Saturday, I heard the tragic news that Kai had died. On Sunday, Kai would have been 16 years old. On Monday, Kai's parents sent in a wonderful birthday cake into school, one that I know Kai would have loved and he would have been reluctant to share it. Amy had already decorated cherry class, preparing for Kai's party. This is an incredibly sad time, we feel shocked, we still can't believe that we have lost such a wonderful young man, who brought such joy to the world.

To have known Kai was to have known a very special young man.

To have known Kai was to have known someone who was very gentle.

To have known Kai was to have known someone who was very brave.

To have known Kai was to have known someone who was determined.

To have known Kai was to have known someone who loved the simple pleasures of life - especially food.

To have known Kai was to have known someone who inspired others to do things that they wouldn't otherwise have done - even to write a book.

To have known Kai was to have known someone who brought out the best in people.

To have known Kai was to have known someone who brought enormous love into the world.

You were a very lucky person if you were to have known Kai.

I cannot ever remember hearing Kai cry, it was something he rarely did – unless something serious happened like having to wait too long at McDonald's.

So, for the next few minutes we will follow Kai's example - try to dry our tears and celebrate an all too short, but very special life, and remember how privileged we all were to have known Kai.

I felt an overwhelming sense of pride, I felt so proud that this boy, who was ours, had such an impact on so many people. Funny stories were told, as well as memories made. I left the school for the last time that day feeling a mixture of pride and overwhelming sadness, and a cold sharp shock of reality.

Donation pages started to pop up online, Liz and Vicky had set one up to help with the cost of Kai's funeral, Terri Rustil also set one up to make memories with the kids and bring back smiles to their faces. I was overwhelmed with how much people loved Kai, flowers and gifts were still arriving every single day. Scott was in panic mode and dragging every single quad bike and motor bike out of his shed, he cleaned them and listed them for sale. He felt sick that he had to get rid of his precious bikes that Kai loved to go on, but we needed the money especially for Kai's funeral. He needed the best, he deserved the best.

Scott sold every single last one of his prized possessions and I watched in despair and guilt that he had to do this. He still wasn't working, he couldn't leave me, and his mind wasn't on the job. Bills still needed to be paid, food bought, everything was carrying on as before, yet our world ended. There was no support or help for us on offer, we had no one to turn to, and we're too proud to ask. We estimated Kai's funeral would come to at least £6000, we were also thousands of pounds down from the lack of income. I had phoned all the relevant departments to make them aware that Kai had died. Of course, Kai's bus was a Motability van, that had to go, we had the option of buying it, but we didn't have the £8,750 needed to do so.

I felt sick at the thought of handing Kai's bus back, yes it was only a van, but it held so many special memories to us. The first time we got it, the look of joy on Kai's face when he realised he had his own lift, holidays, appointments, all of us together in Kai's bus. Scott had made up half of the amount, but we had to pay for Kai's funeral which added together, and the cost of living, we needed £16,000 to sort us out. I didn't care about money, I accepted the bus was going to be handed back, Scott wouldn't, and he was selling all he had to keep it.

Beckie, aware of our situation with the bus, rang me crying. I couldn't get any sense out of her and had to wait until she had calmed down. My confusion turned to shock when I realised her cries were happy cries, her brother, Andrew, had phoned her, at the wrong time for her as she was upset. She explained that our bus was going back and how Scott should be grieving and instead was trying to come up with the money needed to buy it. Andrew had told her he had the money, he would loan it to us so we could buy the bus until we were back on our feet, he couldn't think of a nicer way to use his money.

Scott and I cried, we were shocked and full of gratitude, we declined as we couldn't accept it. Andrew phoned and said the money was going into our account whether we liked it or not, and to stop thinking about it now, to concentrate on each other and the kids. We brought Kai's bus! I cannot explain how much this meant to the both of us, and still to this day I don't think Andrew understands what a kind beautiful thing he did when we were at our lowest. When Scott returned to work he worked as hard as he could and paid back every penny within a few months.

Kai's funeral was booked for 6th March, I couldn't even think straight. Jodie helped to phone around organising things for me that I couldn't do myself. The simplest tasks were huge to me now. Even reading a simple email would send me into a huge rage, and I would give up. Hailey set about organising the wake, and Beckie and Wendy sorted the food. I didn't have to do a single thing other than say yes or no to things they asked. Everything was taken out of my hands, I said what I wanted, and they did it all. Scott and I had booked and organised everything funeral wise, apart from the coffin, I couldn't bring myself to do it. Beckie did it for me, I told her exactly what I wanted, and she did the rest. We had decided on white for everything, we wanted the kids to be as less scared as possible, I asked for

129

everyone to come wearing something white. The coffin would be not coffin shaped, and would be white, covered in pictures of us with Kai. On the top I wanted a crown with 'King Kai' and his full name underneath it. I wanted a big celebration party of Kai's life after, for the children, because I didn't want it to be in a dark pub with everyone sitting around. I wanted the kids to be up dancing and having fun, and to look back and see their last memory of their brother as a happy one. I ordered a McDonalds wreath along with a Peter Pan one, which Beckie paid for. A son, grandson and brother wreath, and a cushion with a crown and Kai's name on. All in white, apart from the McDonalds flowers.

I sent out this message –

Kai's funeral will be held at St Katharine's church in Ickleford, Hitchin at 2.30pm on 6th March. This is a short service, we will then be heading to Holwell crematorium, Bedford Road, Hitchin straight after for a longer service. This will be about Kai and his life, afterwards we will then have a celebration of Kai's life with a party at Arlesey football club, which will be open for you and your children to attend. We ask that everyone wears white in some form, trousers, jeans, skirt, whichever you want but no suits or dark suits. Kai was the light in our lives and dark does not represent that. EVERYONE is welcome, we just ask that children only attend the celebration of life party afterwards. The party is centred around children and will include a disco and entertainment so please feel free to have them there. This is going to be the hardest day of our lives and I know that those of you that loved Kai will also be sad. This is an open invite

130

so please feel free to bring who you want to support you. Scott and Vikki x

SOMEWHERE OVER THE RAINBOW

With Kai's post mortem now complete, we were waiting for the results. Kai was still in the hospital which distressed me so much. I wanted him in the chapel of rest, so we could spend time with him and see him as much as we could before his funeral. After many more fuck ups, due to one thing and another, Kai was not released until days before his funeral. I felt cheated out of the opportunity to see my son, as well as for family and friends who now didn't have the opportunity to say their goodbyes. It took many phone calls, and crying and shouting, until we finally got the call to say Kai was on his way to the funeral home, which was around the corner from us. I knew he was coming home that day as it had started to snow at the very same time Kai was placed into the car for his journey home.

Scott's friend Lincoln, who has a printing business, printed some loving memory keepsake cards for us. We had Kai smiling on his new decking placed on them with a picture of Peter Pan underneath followed by the words – *'You know that place between sleep and awake, the place where you can still remember dreaming? That's where I'll always love you. That's where I'll be waiting.'* He did a huge box load to hand out at no cost. Hailey, who organised the hall, managed to get it for free when she explained what it was for. The disco factory also slashed some money off and threw in a candy floss machine and entertainment free of charge. We learnt that he was one of Scott's customers and had realised who the funeral was for and had called Hailey back with his lovely offer. Wendy, Ria's Auntie, helped Beckie to prepare the food at no cost, we just paid for the food. Beckie spent hours and hours preparing food and making a huge photo board full of Kai and his loved ones. I was oblivious to all of this at the time, living life in my safety bubble. Friends helped set up the hall, Beckie ordered and sorted out the balloons for the balloon release. I literally told them what I wanted, gave them the money and they sorted the whole party for us. My friend and hair dresser Kelly, from Style Me, closed her shop for the night and did my hair while Beckie sat with me. It felt wrong having my hair done but wanted to look my best for Kai. He loved my hair and would always sit sucking it and twirling it around his fingers. When I went to pay Kelly she wouldn't accept, I don't think she knows how much it meant to me, to be alone in the shop without worrying I would bump into someone I knew.

Scott ordered some personalised number plates for the van with Kai's name on, which the children loved so much, he also ordered some little 'King Kai' stickers to go on the windows. Our tattooist, and very dear friend Andy West, drew some beautiful portraits of Kai that we will treasure forever. He also sent us the videos of him drawing them. He really is such a good friend to Scott. Again, I don't think he understands how much those pictures mean to us, he did tell us that he loved having time to draw our boy and it really got him.

The results came through the post, the last few months of waiting to see if I had a brain tumour, only to find out it wasn't. Now I had to find out if it was cervical cancer. I picked the letter up and, as horrid as this sounds, I prayed hard it was cancer. This could be my way out, I could be with Kai again. I opened the letter to the results saying my smear test was normal. This sent me into a deeper depression, I didn't care, I just wanted to be with Kai. After speaking to the doctor, it turned out that the pill I was on was causing all my problems, the bleeding, no hormones in my body and my head aches. It was agreed, as mentioned previously, I would come off the pill as my body wasn't reacting well to it. Scott, Beckie and Terri were over the moon, no more tests. All I could think was that was my way out of this misery.

Kai was now at the chapel of rest and we arranged to go and see him. I needed to see him, as after all the hold ups I still convinced myself they were hiding something from me. Were his organs taken? Was it really Kai laying there? Writing this down I sound mad, but at the time they were very real fears of mine, and however irrational it seemed I needed to know for sure. Clint, Hannah, Brett and Terri all came with us to see Kai. We got there and waited to see Kai, only to be told that his coffin had to stay closed. We were told this might mean he was unviewable, we were devastated. Scott begged and pleaded to be able to see Kai, he sobbed and raged but it made no difference. I went home more convinced than ever that something wasn't right. Hailey phoned to see how I was feeling after seeing Kai and once I explained what had happened she was raging. She phoned them back at once and demanded an explanation, that's the thing with Hailey, she won't just take no for an answer! Once everything had been explained it turned out to be a mix up, someone had written on the form closed coffin, as I hadn't been sure I wanted to see Kai again. No one was to blame and considering how lovely the funeral company had been to us we didn't hold it against them. Hailey arranged for us to be able to see Kai the following day.

The schools had been amazing, Lola's nursery had her for extra days as and when we needed which went right up until July. Nothing was too much, and they went out of their way to be supportive and as helpful as they can be. I can never thank them enough for helping me in those early days. The girls and Bailey were still having counselling and the schools were in constant contact keeping me updated with how they were. Again, nothing was too much to ask of them at my girl's school and they continue to be supportive to this day.

The day we could see Kai was going to be the very last time I saw my baby, it started to snow as soon as we got into the car, and 'Missing You' started to play on the radio. We pulled up and with heavy hearts walked in to spend our last moments with our beautiful blue eyed giant. Kai was laying with his arms on his chest, he looked perfect, it had been nearly 5 weeks since he died. His face looked so much more peaceful, but his nose didn't look like Kai's anymore, it looked smaller and a little squashed. He was now in his green Puma hoody, which made me smile as Donna said he would get his own way. I had asked for him to be in his blue hoody as I liked the colour, he always suited blue. Seeing him in his green hoody I left it at that, Kai had won, he wanted the green one on and for some reason that had happened. I felt sick that this was my last ever moment with my boy, Terri, Scott and I stood together not quite understanding how this could have happened.

The day of Kai's funeral arrived, and the snow had started to melt away, only light frostings were still present. I didn't want anyone back at my house, I couldn't face people. I still found it hard to see people especially all at once, I still felt judged and pure guilt. I didn't sleep a wink and laid watching the clock, listening to the rhythm of the hands turning. The children were also in a quiet mood. We had decided Lola was far too young to be at the funeral, so Beckie collected her and took her to Michaela's, her niece, house until it was time for the party which she would attend. I didn't want to move, I wanted to lay in bed and let the day pass me by. Scott, as ever, was in charge and took care of us all that day. Terri had gone back home a couple of weeks before hand. I lay in Kai's room looking at his medal still sitting on his shelf, his aftershave and bottles of smellies, and his hats. Still untouched in the same place. Weeks before I had tried to buy some more of Kai's favourite aftershave 'Best' by Calum Best. It was now discontinued, I shared a post online asking if anyone knew where it was stocked. The next thing I know, Calum Best had added me on Facebook and in boxed me and arranged for boxes to be sent to our home, along with his condolences. I can never thank people, or him, enough for giving me my boy's smell back, and enough of it to last a very long time. We got up and sat in silence, even the kids didn't talk. Soon it was time to get ready, the girls had matching white lace dresses with their white frilly ankle socks and boots, along with a light pink furry coat to keep out the chilly air. Bailey had navy Chinos and a crisp white Lacoste shirt to match his dad's navy Chinos and Ralph Lauren shirt. I wore a white lace dress, and a baby blue powdered coat, which now hung off me, along with boots. We didn't look like we were going to a funeral which was exactly how I wanted it to be. My brother, Thomas, and his partner, Sharlene, arrived at our home, and spent a couple of hours with us, which I am forever thankful for as it was a distraction. I had spent the morning lying in bed refusing to go, Scott had to talk me into it.

Standing outside our home waiting for the horses and carriage to arrive was very hard, this would be the last time our son would be home with us. Thomas and Sharlene had left minutes before to meet us at the church. My friend, Abi, was already outside taking discreet photos as we had asked her to, so Lola could later look back at the day. Soon we heard the clip clop of horses and walking ahead was the undertaker in a top hat and long coat. The horses were even more beautiful in reality, brilliant white with pale blue plumed feathers cascading from their heads. The carriage behind them held my boy, in his forever bed, surrounded by photos of happy memories. Inside his coffin he had his personal letters from all of us, along with his be brave bear and photos. The horses turned around to face the correct way to the church, pausing for a few moments to allow us to gather our thoughts. We climbed into the waiting car behind, Scott looked haunted, and the kids held onto our hands as the car started up and we headed to the church. Abi still snapping away in the background.

As we made our way to the church, people stopped, heads bowed. Cars gave way and saluted in respect, there was only one guy that was inpatient and over took the horses, he later wrote a long letter of apology. Pulling up, I could see crowds of people making their way into the church, I felt sick. I didn't want to get out of the car until everyone was inside, I felt that if people were waiting to see me and speak to me I wouldn't make it into the church. I needed to focus and concentrate on what I was here for. Beckie made sure everyone was seated, we waited a while not speaking, sitting in silence not sure of what to do next. We each got out of the car, and slowly walked towards the church, my legs suddenly felt heavy, I felt the weakest I had ever felt in my life. The short path felt like a huge effort to walk up, Kai was ahead of us being carried. I didn't look up, I knew that looking up would stop me from going into the church. I kept my head down and made my way in, each of us holding hands for support. Sam Smith's 'Lay Me Down' started to echo around the church as we made our way inside. Kai had always loved Sam Smith and it felt wrong and out of place, usually he would be rocking, shouting, and dancing along, now there was silence. I didn't look up, I walked slowly, watching my feet, to make sure they were still moving as I made my way to my seat. I couldn't see anyone as the tears in my eyes blocked my view, I looked ahead and noticed that a teacher from every year at the girl's school were standing in front of me to the side, as were teachers from Lola's nursery and Kai's school. I was overwhelmed with emotion that they had come to support my children, and us as a family. I stood as some words were said from the Reverend and Sam Smith faded off into the background. I could hear sobs and sniffles all around me, as my senses were over loaded with emotions. Matthew's gospel chapter 18: verses 1-5 and 10 were read out. After, Beckie stood to give her reading, I could see her struggling to hold it all together, she had been so strong I could tell that at any moment she was ready to break. She stood swaying and holding onto to the stand for support as she read from her paper words she had carefully chosen, first reading a poem she had found and then her own words:

You're one of Heaven's angels now, a perfect little star. And when you shine the world can see, how beautiful you are. May you fly with magic wings, on clouds so soft and white. May your heart be joyful,

139

and your days bathed in light. And though our hearts are broken, and your life was far too short. We thank you, sweetest angel, for the happiness you brought.

I first met Vikki and Kai at Wonderland Nursery, she wasn't that keen on me at first but then we were teamed up together, so she had little choice. The day I met the blonde haired bright-eyed little boy, I knew I was going to fall in love with him. Once Kai had settled into nursery life, he loved it. Even if you couldn't see him, you would always hear him getting into mischief, and the giggling coming from Joanie, Carly and Ria. Our friendship blossomed, and I would visit regularly. Scott and Vikki asked if I would become Kai's carer, I was honoured as I knew just how precious Kai was to them. I gained their trust and was able to take Kai out, we had some lovely times together and I have so many wonderful memories of us together. But the one that really stands out for me is the day Mum and I took Kai to Skegness. We had a lovely day, Kai ate non -stop, going on the beach and having a donkey ride. On the way home on the train there was a family opposite us enjoying their picnic, of course Kai spotted this and stood in the aisle trying to help himself. Eventually, they gave in to his puppy dog eyes and shared with him. When Bailey was old enough to speak he began to call me Nan. On many occasions I was asked if Vikki was my daughter! When the girls came along they carried this on, but no not Kai, he would shout at the top of his voice, "Beck!" This would often mean he wanted a bath or something to eat! Kai was one of the most loving, happiest, bravest boys, I have ever had the pleasure of knowing. No matter what life threw at him he would always be smiling. He had the most infectious laugh and wicked sense of humour. If you hurt yourself, swore, or someone was being told off he would always laugh at their misfortune. The last thing that I said to Kai was, "Mummy tells me you have been climbing and being a sod. Now get down Kai, stop climbing and be good." All I could hear was Kai belly laughing down the phone. I feel incredibly blessed to have been a part of Kai's life, he taught me so many things. The most important being it is ok not to be ok. Thank you, Kai, for being you. - ***Beckie***

I was so proud she had managed to read, she did us all proud, her voice cracked with emotion, but she got through it. We sat and said our prayers, I was still battling with God and found this hard because I felt he had let me down, let us all down. I was so very cross, yet still couldn't bare not to have him mentioned. We stood to sing 'He's Got the Whole World In His Hands', I gripped onto the pew in front of me, my legs wobbled, and I was sure my legs would give away at any moment. I was broken, but I held it all inside even though I wanted to rage and scream that this wasn't fair, I wanted to go over to the coffin and make sure he was tucked in right, inside. Instead I stood sobbing, my throat hurt, and my head was pounding. We exited the church to Mariah Carey's 'Butterfly' song, I felt hands squeezing my shoulder and stroking my arm as I walked out of the church, again not looking up. As Kai was placed into the car to head to the crematorium I stopped and looked for the first time, there were so many people. I wanted to thank each and every one of them, so Scott and I cuddled everyone on the way out. I wanted to show how much it meant to us that they were with us on such a hard day.

We arrived at the crematorium and as we did the cold air stopped to make way for the sun. People were stood taking their coats off as the heat hit them. We sat in the car waiting for the go ahead to go inside. As we waited people started to cry out and point, I was in my own world and my sister, Katie, ran over to the car, "Vikki, look over there." She pointed, and I looked up to see the biggest rainbow that lit up the whole of the grounds of the crematorium. I was sure it was a message from Kai, 'look Mummy I am OK.' There wasn't a dry eye as everyone stopped and stared at the rainbow which had come from nowhere. Abi stood snapping away with her camera.

We entered the crematorium to Sam Smith's 'Lay Me Down'. Kai's forever bed was placed in front of us with his '*SON*' flowers gently placed at the floor. A video montage of photos I had carefully handpicked with Scott played on a loop in the background the whole way through. Kai's teacher took her place and gave her reading:

To have known Kai was to have known a young man with sheer determination and bravery. A young man who was so full of life. From the outset Kai presented himself as a very different young man. Once you got to know and understand Kai you got to recognise the various depths of his character. Being Kai's teacher meant that I was fortunate to know this side of him. A young man who could run faster than you would ever have expected. A young man who had a wonderful sense of humour: he had the most infectious laugh which would always brighten up your day. A young man with the cheekiest smile which is so perfectly reflected on the last page of the order of service. A young man who was extremely gentle and so very happy with the little things in life.

Most of the time when you wanted Kai to do something it wasn't for his lack of understanding, but more due to the fact he had his own ideas about what he wanted to do or didn't want to do in many cases! And why shouldn't he be able to express this, after all he was a typical teenager! Once you had sussed out Kai's passions, food and music, it's incredible just how motivated he could be!

One of my favourite memories of Kai was when he was sat at the table while I was preparing snack. I had plated up a sausage roll each on the side and began to start handing them out to the students. When I walked back over I couldn't work out how I didn't have enough. It wasn't until I looked over and saw Kai sat there making his way through three sausage rolls that I realised he had got up from his chair, walked over to where I was making snacks and had helped himself, and then casually walked sat back down! I laughed and then thought to myself, well what can I say? We do strive for independence!

I remember the first educational health care plan meeting I had with Vikki where we discussed new learning intentions for Kai. I still remember to this day walking out of the meeting and thinking, wow, a real-life superwoman, a mother who

143

completely gets her son, one who understands. A family who have four other children but somehow find the energy within them to ensure the very best for Kai.

When you work with children and young adults with special educational needs people often say, "I don't know how you do it, you deserve a medal." But it really made me think. I chose this career path, I chose to become a teacher and I chose to go into special education. People like Vikki and Scott didn't choose this path, however, their journey through life blessed them with the most wonderful son, and it is these types of people who are the real inspiration. I would like to thank Kai for the joy and laughter that he brought to cherry class, for teaching me to never set the bar too low, for teaching me patience, not just at work but in my own personal life. For opening my eyes to different learning styles and techniques and for teaching me that one sausage roll at snack time is never enough!

It is Kai who has been the real teacher to many! I know that I speak on behalf of myself and all my colleagues at Greenside when I say how saddened we are not to see Kai around the school. He has touched so many of our hearts in so many ways and we will forever be grateful for his presence. It was both an honour and a privilege. A beautiful soul taken from us too soon, but one we will cherish for a lifetime. Sleep tight, until we meet again. Love Amy xxx

Amy's voice cracked with emotion as she laughed and cried her way through her words. The visual

144

tribute continued to play as Kai's song 'Fix You' by Coldplay came on. I was suddenly back at home, Kai on my lap, me singing him his favourite song, "I will try to fix you," as I stroked and kissed his face. Tears streamed down my cheeks as I remembered fondly how much the song meant to us both. Now, it was my turn to do a reading, everyone had told me I didn't have to, no one expected it of me, but I wanted to, I owed it to Kai. He was brave his whole life, I had to be brave at the hardest time of *my* life. I stood and walked past my devastated children and took Scott's hand, we stood together as I read aloud:

The day you came home with us, it snowed, the day you left us, it snowed. You were the most caring, gentle, loving and kindest most beautiful soul, and we were the proudest to know that you were ours. You taught us things we never would have known, you brought people into our lives we never would have met. You took us on a journey we will never forget.

Everything you went through you never once complained, cried or showed any kind of distress. You are the biggest inspiration and we are proud to call you our son. The day you died a part of us died with you, not a minute goes by that you are not in our thoughts, we only spent four nights apart in all your years. You were the funniest, cheekiest boy and although you had very limited speech you told us a thousand words with your eyes. I miss our cuddles, 'elf style' we called them as you were so big and loved to show off how tall you were.

Your pleasures in life were simple, love cuddles, baths and food. We still cannot believe you are not here with us. Every day without you feels like one long nightmare. You changed the world Kai, you may not have known it, but you changed the world of all of those that met you. You tried everything in life possible, from quadding with Daddy, to rollercoasters with Mummy, and to even what balloons taste like, to flirting with nurses.

The children miss you standing in front of the TV and shouting through their favourite shows so they couldn't hear them. We miss you standing above us and laughing at how small we were compared to you. Our 'BFG' we called you, as well as our very own 'Peter Pan'. That's where I imagine you Kai, in Never Never Land. Never having to grow old and exploring everything you can.

Every day I would smother you in kisses and stroke every inch of your beautiful face and tell you, "We couldn't have made you more beautiful and perfect if we had tried." You would smile that smug smile because you knew that, and we would sit and sing your song 'Fix You', to you.

*You may be a star now, and after having so many named after you, you will soon be taking over the sky. Every night we look out and wave at you with your brother and sisters. Some people never get to meet their hero, I was lucky; I gave birth to mine. You may be a star now, but you will forever be my King and I will forever be your Queen. Sleep tight my beautiful boy and fly high. - **Mummy and Daddy***

The children also had their readings read out (see chapter In Loving Memory) which brought tears and laughter from everyone. The committal was read out, as the undertakers all stood around Kai and bowed their heads and Ronan Keating's 'When You Say Nothing at All' played in the background. The song we had playing at our very first scan of Kai, was now the song he would be leaving the world to. The curtains closed, and I knew that this was the last time I would feel my boy around me.

My body was overcome with tiredness and I felt so weak and light. I wanted to scream that this wasn't right, to check on him one last time, to make sure he was dead. Instead I sobbed into my tissue, as a chorus of cries broke out all around me. Kai's pictures continued to flash in the background as we made our way outside. I was swamped with kind words, cuddles and comfort as we stood watching Scott, Harry and our children releasing the white doves into the sky. No words were said as we watched the doves swoop through the air elegantly.

People had come from all over the UK to be there for us, I will never forget it. I got to meet Kristy and Sam, friends I had known online but had never actually met before. I was overcome with emotion that people had stopped their lives for that day to be at our side, I will never forget it.

We drove to Kai's celebration of life party. I had no idea what to expect as I hadn't prepared or had any involvement in the arrangements, only my say so. I walked in to a beautifully decorated hall. Kai's photos on a big board, a big McDonald's balloon arch that Hailey and her friend had spent days making stood behind the DJ she had also arranged.

The food went on for miles with all Kai's favourites, chicken nuggets, quiche, sandwiches and cakes. Wendy and Beckie had done it all and I felt so overcome. 'King Kai' balloons that Beckie and Dot had brought and arranged, floated in the air. It was as perfect as I had dared hope for.

We spent the night watching the children blow bubbles into the air, dance, eat candy floss and shovel cakes into their mouths. Some of Kai's friends were there, dancing with their teachers. Paula and Nick were there with their buckets for William's Wishes charity as I had requested donations to go to their charity. Suddenly, Bette Midler's 'Wind Beneath My Wings' started to play as we made our way outside.

We stood clutching a white balloon each, some had written messages on theirs. After a countdown we released the balloons into the still night sky, no one talking, everyone in their own thoughts. I stood looking at everyone, Kai would have loved this I thought to myself.

At the end of the night Hailey handed the children a letter each, telling them they were off to make new memories at one of Kai's favourite places, Chessington. She had arranged it through a charity Once Upon A Smile, a hotel and weekend at the park just like we had with Kai a few years back. What an amazing thing to have done for us.

FINDING A WAY

Over the next few weeks we would find feathers in the strangest of places, the kids loved finding them and got so excited they started collecting them in a jar. They took them as a sign from Kai, we would walk outside to find them floating mid-air, or placed in places Kai spent time. Even in his room, on my bed.

We now had to decide what to do with Kai's ashes, the more we thought about it the more distressed it made us. I couldn't bear to part with them, and although the crematorium was only behind our house it still felt too far.

Scott was now back at work and worried he wouldn't get the time he needed to sit and talk with Kai. He then came up with an idea, what about a memorial garden right here in our home? The more I thought about it the more I liked the idea. Scott and his friend, Dave, set to work. He was up at 5.00am in the garden, out to work at 9.00am, back home at 5.00pm and then in the garden until 11.00pm.

Scott didn't stop those few weeks, even the rain didn't put a stop to the work him and Dave put in. We got the call to collect Kai's ashes. I cannot explain what it feels like to be handed the child you carried for 9 months, the child you nurtured through illness, kissed away their tears, loved so hard and shared so many good times with to be handed to you in a small box. I felt empty and completely broken. It seemed like we had nothing to look forward to, just more pain and heartache.

Finally, after months of phoning, checking and harassing the poor coroner we had Kai's results back. Kai didn't suffocate, there was no evidence of a seizure, he had simply gone to sleep and died of SUDEP. He didn't feel a thing, his organs were fine, there was no contributing factors, and nothing could have prevented his death. A huge weight felt like it had been lifted from my shoulders, the blame, the guilt and the anger at myself eased a little. Although, to this day I still feel that pang of what if, and I feel so sad he was alone, but I have come to terms with the fact that nothing I, or anyone, did or didn't do would have stopped this from happening.

I had always been a firm believer in us being born with an age we were to die, and nothing would stop that from happening. As horrendous as it was that Kai passed away the day before his 16th birthday, I take comfort in the thought that he died forever young. A real-life Peter Pan.

I shook and cried for weeks after getting Kai's results, I felt anger that I hadn't known anything about SUDEP. I felt like a huge secret had been kept from me, although I now know not that many consultants have come across SUDEP.

This is my one reason for writing this book, to raise as much awareness and funding for a little-known killer in epilepsy. More needs to be done, more needs to be looked into. How can anyone go to bed and simply just not wake up? It makes no sense and I still struggle to this day to understand and make sense of it all. When we found out, Scott took my face in his hands and looked me in the eye, "You were never to blame no matter what the results were, I couldn't have asked for a better mother to my boy. He worshipped you, and you him."

The school my girls attend did a 'wear something white' day in memory of Kai, which was such a lovely kind thing to do. All the donations raised went to William's Wishes. Walking to the school, and seeing all the children in white, and that some had written 'King Kai' on their tops, was overwhelming.

I remember standing with Jay, both of us tearful at the kindness of others. Many people did such kind things for us. Kelly asked for donations at her wedding for TSC and my friends company did a charity event for TSC. My friend, Jan, asked for donations instead of birthday gifts and donated it to TSC. The kindness in people is so overwhelming when you've had something terrible happen to you.

Soon the garden was complete, Scott had fenced off a section with an arch and a gate, all painted in cream. We had a big bench area with shelter and a plaque with Kai's picture and name on.

Plants ran up either side, Kai's swing chair he spent every summer on was now painted seagrass green and cream with a plaque. A star planter with an acer plant, that Nicola brought me, sits in the centre. Then we have a water fountain, right next to a handmade throne that Scott made from scratch out of wood. Placed in the seat are my baby's ashes, on top sits a black stone with Peter Pan quotes and pictures. Every other week someone brings a new plant, a crown, a candle, ornament or bunting around to place in Kai's garden. We sit up there often playing Kai his music, talking to him and sitting thinking about the boy who changed the world.

We didn't get to register Kai's death until 27th April 2018, it was heart-breaking sitting there watching couples walk in happy and giddy with excitement, baby in the car seat ready to register a new life into the world. I sat still, not moving, with the jealousy bubbling away inside of me. Why are they allowed to be happy? Why are we here for the very opposite reasons?

People see me coping and think that I am ok, the truth is I am not, nor will I ever be. I hide it all, to make people feel less uncomfortable, I sit and listen to the moans and gripes about their life, when inside I am thinking I would trade you in an instant.

Kai's death has left such a huge hole in my life, one that nothing will ever fill. People often ask me if I would ever consider having another baby. The answer is no, I would be selfish to, my family was perfect, and it will never be the same. Adding a child to it that didn't know Kai would feel wrong, like I am moving on, I never want to move on, I am stuck here until I am with my boy again.

People say I am brave, they don't see the panic attacks I have at night, the lack of sleep, the forcing myself to get out of bed, to eat, and to get dressed. They don't understand the battles I face every day, when I get a pack of tablets out of the cupboard to ease my head ache, and battle with myself not to take the whole box to stop the pain for good. The anger that comes from nowhere, the rage that boils up inside of you until you explode. I got out of my car and screamed and tried to fight a man in a road rage incident a few months after Kai passed away. Every single bit of rage I had I wanted to take it out on him, I ended up screaming in the street, "Come on then," like a crazy woman, threatening everyone that tried to intervene, before breaking down and getting back in the van and punching the steering wheel repeatedly while screaming.

Some days when I wake up I pretend that Kai is at school and I get on with my day. Other days I can't pretend no matter how much I try, I often leave early to get the kids, so I can scream at the side of the road in my van. I have tried depression tablets, but I don't feel they work for me, nothing is going to change by taking them, Kai still won't be here. I am currently having counselling through CRUSE, who have been amazing. My children are also having intensive counselling through Stand By Me.

The flashbacks are horrendous, I can be getting on with my day, and then I am back there in Kai's room on my knees screaming. I can be walking through a shop, and his song will come on, and that is me done for the day. I plaster on a smile in front of my friends, I pretend I am ok, but inside I am not, I never will be. The old Vikki is gone forever, replaced by one who I struggle to understand. Every first without Kai hurts so much, Mother's Day, Easter, birthdays. I am dreading the experience of Christmas and Kai's first birthday without him, even though, technically, I have been through his birthday without him my mind was still in complete shock that he'd died just the day before.

No one prepares you for losing a child, and even if you are prepared I don't think you accept it, not fully. The nights I do manage to sleep I dream of Kai, and not always good, sometimes I have nightmares that send me into a panic. I have the same dream, that Kai has died, and I cannot accept it, so I put him into a shopping trolley laying on top of a quilt and push him around. I see people staring and ignore them, Kai is with me and that is all that matters. I usually wake up sweating with my heart racing and can't get back to sleep. Most nights I toss and turn, and one night I turned to find Scott asleep face down in his pillow. I completely freaked out and screamed at him to wake up and turn on his side. I scared Scott so much that night we both laid awake crying.

The constant feeling of being judged, watched, never leaves you. The reminders that there is a person missing is remembered every day, by the empty chair, or the mistake of getting out one plate too many. Life has changed so much, I have so much time on my hands now, time I have never had before. I spend a lot of my time cleaning, not knowing what to do with myself, some days I can meet friends, others I want to be alone and cancel. Big happy events right now are an issue, christenings, weddings. It's hard to see everyone happy when that's not how you feel inside. The only thing we have now is each other and our memories. I was clearing out my cupboards and found a huge stash of video recordings, ones I had taken from when Kai was a baby to more recent. I had them all converted and have hours of video of Kai and my children together, I am so thankful I always had a camera in my hand.

Donna gave us another reading, I told her the wood and the digging made sense in the end, it was Kai's garden. Of course, she knew that, but didn't want to sway us by putting it in our heads. I told her that Kai had got his way and had his green hoody on that he wanted. She asked me if we had any signs, I told her we did, Kai's light box that said, 'King Kai' had lit up in the night two nights in a row. When I checked it, the batteries were dead. Donna told me Kai was standing waiting in a smart blue shirt, he wanted to be at our vow renewal we had talked about recently and that he thought his garden was the perfect place to do it! I was stunned into silence, Beckie and Scott and I had sat talking about us renewing our vows in Kai's garden the following year. I had told no one. Kai had been listening. She told us that so many people would and had been getting tattoos of Peter Pan, and crowns, which happened to be true. Kai has his tribute on so many people now.

Scott ordered me a beautiful 'ashes into glass' ring, a blue stone with specks of Kai's ashes inside, engraved inside with 'Forever my king'. I wear it every day and will treasure it forever. Kai's toothbrush is still hanging on the bathroom wall, his coat is still on the peg. I find it so hard to believe he won't ever need to use these again, yet I can't bring myself to move them.

With so much time on my hands I really didn't know what to do, although I help run Scott's carpet cleaning business, Extreme Clean, I was used to being rushed off my feet by routines and dirty nappies! I sat staring at the walls, wishing time away, cleaning and waiting for the kids to come home from school. With Lola starting full time school in September I knew this was only going to get worse.

I mentioned to Scott about doing a nail technician course. Half an hour later, equipment was brought and paid for and Scott had drawn up plans to make me a beauty room. He was so relived I wanted to do something with my time, I know how worried he was going to work, leaving me alone all day. I have since booked onto an NVQ Level 3 course and start this year and Scott has completed my beauty room. I often joke to him what if I don't like it? Or, what if I fail? Although I have a BTEC diploma in childcare, going back into childcare is still too raw. I also feel I am not ready to mix with people on a daily basis and that working from home would be a perfect distraction. I have always loved special needs children, but, again, it is too raw, but who knows what the future holds? Maybe in time this is something I could go back into.

I had a knock on the door after Kai's funeral, two neighbours I hadn't really spoken to much were standing there. In their arms was a love heart cushion with a picture of Kai and me. I was blown away, that they had taken time from their own lives to think of such a lovely gesture. I have got to know Stacey and Debbie this year, and class them as very good friends. They have looked after me, dragged me out and made me live some sort of life at least. I am so very blessed to have such a wonderful circle of friends, good neighbours, and a wonderful family. I know that with their help and support I will keep trying and keep going and doing the best that I can to make my boy proud. I know that I am not perfect, how I deal with things sometimes is not right or wrong, but it is my way. I am doing the best that I can to get through the darkest moment of my life. I am trying to keep standing, trying to be good mum, wife and friend. I don't always get it right, and I am thankful that I have such an amazing support network around me. They never judge, they just listen.

I am bitter about how we were treated over the years, I feel Kai was failed in life and in death. I could have sued so many people so many times, but what would that achieve? Nothing would have changed. I am angry that we were left with no support, only Beckie here to help us a couple of times a week. I am sad we were left to struggle with no equipment, and that every single service we tried to access we were met with 'no funding' or 'doesn't meet the criteria'. I am angry we weren't prepared for Kai to die. I feel we would have spent more time getting on with life and wasted less time fighting.

I am livid we were told we didn't need any outside help by those we trusted. I feel the process of when a child dies needs to change, we had months of fighting and phone calls to find out basic information. I feel everyone involved should have had full training and experience, as I later found out this wasn't the case in our instance. Even registering Kai's death was horrid, sitting in the same waiting room as those full of excitement registering a new life. I feel like saying a big 'FUCK YOU' to everyone that failed my son and us, and for those that tried to contact me and be nice when he died yet wouldn't give us the time of day when we needed them when Kai was here. I could have gone deeper into how we were failed, but I want this to be about Kai's life, and raising awareness of SUDEP. We were failed, and it makes me feel sick to my stomach to know that others are still being failed. I feel angry that as a family because Kai was fed, cleaned and looked after, we were left unsupported. We did it, but my boy deserved the world and they failed him.

People say I am brave to still be standing, but what choice do I have? If I wasn't here what would Scott and my children do? How would they get through life without Kai and me? I don't want Kai to be remembered in a way which would be damaging, I want him to be remembered for being fearless, brave, funny and inspiring, everything I wish I could be. The day I found my boy forever asleep will be with me for the rest of my life, no amount of counselling, anti-depressants, or anything else is going to erase that image. The hole in our lives he has left will never be filled. All we can do now is keep trying, keep standing, and stay strong together.

People often ask me if I would have wanted to know about SUDEP, the answer is yes. We know the risks of cancer, we talk about cancer even when the prognosis isn't good. Yet SUDEP is kept hidden like a dirty secret. It breaks my heart all over again when I hear in the news someone else has died from SUDEP, knowing full well their parents probably had no idea, like me. I wish I would have known Kai was only here for a short time, I would have made his last few weeks as best as I could. I only take comfort in the fact that he died knowing that he was loved, by everyone. He knew I loved him with all I had, and I knew he loved me. He went to bed laughing and that is my last memory of my little Peter Pan.

Thank you to everyone who read about Kai, who knew him, or who felt like they did. For following our journey, through the good times and the bad. For laughing and crying with us. For supporting us and keeping us going. For loving my boy as hard as you did.

Thank you.
Vikki x

NOTE: All proceeds from the sale of my three "Fall" books will be donated to SUDEP Action, registered charity number 1164250. Please read on for a note from them.

A WORD FROM SUDEP

What is epilepsy?

Epilepsy is one of the most common and serious neurological conditions, affecting over half a million people in the UK alone (1 in every 103 people). At least 87 people are diagnosed with epilepsy every day in the UK. It is thought that one in five people will experience a seizure at some point in their lives. There are over 40 different types of epilepsy, and it can develop in anyone at any time of life.

Is epilepsy serious?

Epilepsy is a serious long -term condition, and unfortunately a number of people with epilepsy do die each year. Epilepsy is in the top ten of all causes of death in people under 70; there are approximately 1,000 epilepsy related deaths every year (at least 21 deaths a week). Most of these sudden deaths are in young and otherwise healthy people.

Most epilepsy deaths are because of accidents, suicide, status epilepticus (a continuous seizure which lasts 30 minutes or more) and Sudden Unexpected Death in Epilepsy (SUDEP).

Many people with epilepsy live long, healthy lives but it is important to know about epilepsy risks, as there are often simple, positive steps which can be taken to reduce risk and stay safer.

What is SUDEP?

Sudden Unexpected Death in Epilepsy (SUDEP) is when a person with epilepsy dies suddenly and prematurely and no other cause of death is found. It is not a condition or disease, but rather a useful category for this type of death (which helps aid research and monitoring of deaths).

How can epilepsy risks (including risks linked to SUDEP) be reduced?

It is recommended that people with epilepsy speak with their health professionals about their individual risk levels, as this varies from person to person and can also change over time. As half of all epilepsy deaths are not SUDEP related, they should be aware of all risks related to epilepsy which may cause injury or death.

There are known risk factors linked to epilepsy deaths, some of which are modifiable. We also know that 42% of all epilepsy deaths are potentially avoidable, so it is vital people with the condition know about these risks and how to reduce them where possible.

Whether you're a parent or carer of a person with epilepsy, or a someone living with the condition; it can be worrying to think about the risks of epilepsy. But knowing about risks, discussing them with others (clinicians, family, teachers, etc), and taking steps to reduce them, can help you navigate living well with epilepsy.

Having a long-term condition like epilepsy doesn't mean you can't take part in everyday activities, but it does mean you might need to take some extra steps to make sure you keep as safe as possible.

To help people with epilepsy (as well as their family and their clinicians) better understand, discuss and manage risks, the charity **SUDEP Action** has created free downloadable resources, as well as two free, award winning tools:

SUDEP & Seizure Safety Checklist - a ten-minute checklist for health professional to use with their patients as a review, to support discussions about their epilepsy, wellbeing and risk. Fortified by the latest research into epilepsy deaths, the Checklist is currently used by over 600 health professionals across the UK.

EpSMon - an app that enables people with epilepsy to **self-manage their condition** in between appointments with their health professional. Based on the SUDEP & Seizure Safety Checklist, it is readily accessible via the Apple or Google Play app stores, and now well over 3,500 users! It is also now part of the **NHS Innovation Accelerator Programme** (NIA) to support its development and implementation into the NHS.

It is important to highlight that anyone concerned about their epilepsy, should speak to their health professional(s). It is also vital that you don't make any changes to your epilepsy medication without speaking to them first.

More about SUDEP Action

SUDEP Action (formerly Epilepsy Bereaved) founded in 1995, is dedicated to raising awareness of epilepsy risks and tackling all epilepsy deaths, including SUDEP. They are the **only UK charity specialised in supporting and involving people bereaved by epilepsy**. They also provide free information and tools to help keep people with epilepsy safe.

For more information and resources about epilepsy and how to manage risks, visit www.sudep.org

SUDEP Action **offer support after an epilepsy death**, as well as ongoing support for people where deaths have happened years before. The support team can help those bereaved to understand what they are going through emotionally and can provide free counselling sessions.

163

They also have expertise in helping families with understanding the inquest procedure, death investigations and in supporting families to make sure lessons are learnt after a death. **The Epilepsy Deaths Register**, gives people who have experienced an epilepsy death the opportunity to provide vital information about the death - which informs research and brings us one step closer to finding answers, and learning lessons from epilepsy deaths.

The charity also works with bereaved families across the UK and internationally, to raise awareness and funds to help tackle epilepsy deaths and make sure that every epilepsy death counts.

If you have been affected by an epilepsy death, please contact our free support team on 01235 772852 or email support@sudep.org

IN LOVING MEMORY
SUDEP

Kai John Dean Hammond, 21-1-2002 – 20-1-2018.
Our very own Peter pan, thank you for teaching me
all you did. Thank you for being you. Our hearts are
broken, they will never heal. Until we are together
again. Mummy, Daddy, Bailey, Honey-Mae, Daisy
and Lola. x

Kai Hammond, you were the best brother, and
every night I look up at the stars and hope you come
back to us. I can't believe you have gone, you have
left a big hole in my heart. I will mis my room buddy
when we go on holidays, every day I wake up and
pray it has all been one big nightmare. Life without
you will never be the same. Love Bailey. x

Kai Hammond, I miss you so much, I miss
how when you were a bit younger you would sit in
your wheelchair near the freezer and grab as much
frozen food as you could and quickly ate it. My
favourite memory of you is when you sat on me

instead of next to me even when there was lots of space. I also loved it when you used to grab my neck to give me a hug, that was funny. I love you Kai and I always will. Honey-Mae.

Kai Hammond, I love you so much and I will never forget you, I miss your cheekiness and your cute smile and laugh. My favourite memory is when you used to dance to Sam Smith. I loved it when you would trap me on the sofa for cuddles and kisses. My favourite thing about you was your smile. I love you and I will miss you forever my BFF. Love Daisy.

Kai Hammond, I love and miss you, even though I didn't like you pinning me down for kisses and cuddles I still loved you. You were heavy that's why I didn't like it. I loved your big blue eyes I love you Kai. Love Lola.

***

Owen who died from SUDEP July 2014 aged 39, we miss the good times, laughter and especially your wonderful bear hugs. Sleep tight my beautiful son.

Nikey Robinson passed from SUDEP aged 23, "she who leaves a trail of glitter is never forgotten." Love always, Mum. x

Matthew Dunkley passed away 24th August 2014 aged 24, forever young. I love you Matt, love Mum.

Samantha was 19 when she passed away 16th July 2009. "Ain't no mountain high enough." Keep singing up there, angel. Love Mum, Billy, Adam and Alice.

Alex James, aged 34, who went to heaven on 26th February 2015. Our bright shining star, we miss you so very much. Love Mum, Dad and Luke. x

Our beautiful girl Jodhi Kate Russell grew her angel wings 5th October 2017, aged 17. G'nite sweet cheeks love you to the moon and back. Love from Mum, Danii and Amie. x

Kieran William Lyon, went to help God 18-3-16, aged 19. Miss my best friend and my son so much. Mum. x

Alexandra Reburn aged 30, "With a smile that lights up the darkest days." Love from your Mum and Poke-friends. We miss you.

Alisha Logan, aged 4, died from SUDEP 18-11-07. Love and miss you always and forever. Mum. x

Jemma Louise Radcliffe died from SUDEP 22-5-11 aged 28, miss you so much 'sweet child of mine'. Love you loads from your Mum, sisters and brother. X

My sweet little boy Taylor Leigh Webb sadly taken to young on 26-7-04 aged just 9 years old. Shine bright my beautiful star, as you did in life. Missing you more each passing year. Love you forever until the day we meet again. Mummy. x

Anthony sadly passed away on 29th January 2003 aged 22, I miss him so much. There is not a day that goes by that his sister doesn't say his name. Mam and Jo. x

Heather, taken by SUDEP at the age of 23 on 5-2-15. Love you buggerboo, Mom. X

Jonathan James Zito, taken suddenly at the age of 35 to SUDEP. We love and miss you dearly,

167

our hearts break more every day. Love your Mum and sister, Paula. x

Daniellle Martin was taken away on 30th October 1991 aged 3 and a half years old. Mum. x

Martin Corbett, aged 36, taken by SUDEP 26-5-17.

Stetson Wyatt Rodgers, aged 15, you will always be our sweetest boy ever. X

Natalie 34, re-born an angel 6-9-16, you are my sunlight, moonlight and the air that I breathe. Love Dad. Xx

Marcaylin Fyneena Edelbrock, aged 4, 23-12-13 - 17-5-18. We miss you so much, angel girl. Love Mom, Dad and Sissiy Carys. X

Joshua Kirk Mazurek 1-9-07 aged 22, we love and miss you more than can be expressed in words. Love Mom and Dad. X

Darrian Diaz, 10-19-92 – 1 -11-17, she lost her fight with epilepsy to SUDEP. You will live forever in our hearts and souls, you are missed. Love you.

Hazel Cooper, 25-12-89 – 05-11-07. x

Timothy Francis Collins died from epilepsy from SUDEP 7-8-77 – 5-29-14, aged 36 years old. Miss you dearly Mom, Megan and Erin Christine.

Hayley McGurk, died from SUDEP aged 20, on 20-07-15, just gut wrenchingly awful. X

Kayleigh Nixon, we miss you. 14-12-82 – 5-4-90. Your nieces and nephews never knew your love. SUDEP took care of that. x

Dan Dench, passed from SUDEP aged 35, we miss your smile and your laughter every day, forever loved by his family. Sally Dench. x

168

Claire, sadly passed away 29-11-06 aged 26, miss my daughter so much. Mum. x

Orla Jacqueline Arnell aged 14 years. 11-1-00 – 21-7-14. You light up the skies up above me, a star o bright you blind me. We miss you so much my beautiful squish. Love you always Mummy. x

Joseph Short (Joe Joe cheeky monkey) died 11-3-02 aged 22 months, sleep well little man. Love you. Mum. x

Becky Grace Scrivens. Sunrise 4-8-92 - sunset 4-5-04. Keep your face always towards the sunshine and shadows will fall behind you. We love and miss you so much. X

David Ian Bastian died of SUDEP aged 48, 22-8-15. I miss you so much, Dave please watch over our beautiful children always. Anita. x

Olivia June Mcpherson, 13-2-91 – 13-2-15, forever 24, until I see you again, I hold you tight in my heart my beloved daughter. Mum. x

Crystal Claire Burgoine passed away from SUDEP, 27-5-87 – 22-1-08. An amazing Mummy, Auntie and Sister. Lyndsey. x

Victoria Isabella Rae, 28-10-97 – 6-4-17, forever 19. Miss you more and more every passing day our beautiful girl. Love always from Mum, Dad, and all your family and friends. x

Kory Anthony James Johnson, 21-6-96- 14-2-18, aged 21. Passed over due to SUDEP. We love you Kory and miss you every single day. X

Max Miller Prior, my gorgeous boy, fly with the angels, dance with the stars. 4-8-09 – 21-6-11. Mum. x

Iain Krelle, forever 45, so sorry we didn't get to say goodbye. Julia and family. x

Kerry Jayne Pates, forever 19. Always in our hearts and thoughts, loved and missed more than words can say. Love Mum, Dad, Kieran and all your family and friends. x

Emily Maiya Sumaria, born 24-3-93 - died 4-12-12, aged just 19, love you to the moon and back. x

Thomas James Sinden (TJ), 6-9-90 – 6-9-16, forever 26. Always in our minds and forever in our hearts. Love and miss you every day. Mum, Josh and Neil. x

Justin Phillip Landis, forever 22. 11-22-93 – 2-3-16. Counting down the days until we see you again. Love Mum, Dad and DD. x

Sam Watford taken aged just 14, a whole life lost, and a family left heartbroken and left behind. Always in our thoughts missed and loved forever. Mum. x

Jayne Lyndee Andrews, forever 20. Born 6 July 95 and died 7 January 2016. She is dancing with the angels.

Alex Rivera, born 30-6-95 - died 6-7-16. Missed every day so very much. We were blessed to have you in our world, the world is a better place because of your time here. Love always Mom. x

Rose, 27-4-94 – 08-9-13, taken so suddenly, much loved and missed every minute by all her family. That beautiful kind smile that all of us took for granted. Life will never be the same. x

Jameson Page age 10, Mumma loves you all the way up buggy boy. x

Chrissy aged 29, beloved daughter, sister and aunt. We love and miss your beautiful smile and contagious laugh. With all our love, your family. x

Ismaeel Rahim aged 5, went to the angels on 1-4-17 forever in our thoughts. Love Mum and Dad. x

Damian James Swan, forever 10. Mum, Dad and Kayleah-Ann miss you so much. Keep dancing for those 5 stars in the skies. Tina. x

Grace Mary, forever 20 months. We love and miss you so much, with every breath we take. Love always and forever Mommy, Daddy, Juli, Olivia, Emily and Cole. X

Casey Elizabeth Cordova, forever 32, and forever in our hearts. We love and miss you so very much, my sweet pea girl. x

Erin Elizabeth, gone to heaven 17-9-17. I am still trying to make sense of this illness that came so strong and so sudden. I am doing my best to take care of your three boys, Love you forever, Mom. x

Alan Davies, 28-8-84 – 2-6-15. A much-missed son, always 20. Love you. x

Todd Mitchell Campbell, 20-1-89 – 1-11-11, aged 22 years. "I never thought that when I fell to sleep one night I would wake up and you would be gone forever." X

Georgie Barnes, such a beautiful girl inside and out, taken from us aged 3. Mummy, Daddy and Gracie love you to the moon and back and miss you so very much. x

Georgie Butler, forever in our hearts, loved and missed always. x

Natalie Jane Brown, 8-10-89 – 22-7-17. Love you to the moon and back, forever 27. Love you babes, love Mum and Dad, friends and family. x

Forever you will be baby pea, Penelope Jane Mitchell, 1-5-15 – 30-7-17.

Benjamin David Todd, our precious son went to heaven on 6-4-15, aged 22 years. Always loved, forever missed, until we meet again. Love you, Ben. We miss you so much! Love Mum, Dad, Sarah, Aleisha and Mike, Lucas and Lachlan. x

Vicki, 10-2-13 - aged 26, she left a beautiful permanent reminder, he is now 7. x

Ethan aged 15 months, 31-1-13 – 2-5-14. Loved and missed every day. With all our love Mummy, Daddy, Taylor, Hannah and Evie. x

Shayne Pereira, 8-11-74 – 1-4-2002. Beloved brother who taught me so much about life. Ant.

In loving memory of Michael James Bennett, 3-7-92 – 29-3-15. Our special boy, with love Tracy, Duncan and sister Emma. x

Drew Young, 22 years being awesome, wherever you are. Love always Mam, Dad, Grace and Matthew. x

Joel Christian Paolucci, 12-22-81 -10-4-07, aged 25. You made life happier, funnier and better in every way. Absent from the body, present with the Lord. We miss you always. x

Jordan Meier, 25th July 2018, we celebrate your 30th birthday as we lay you to rest. Missing you every day and knowing you are caring for those who have suffered too and joined you in heaven. Love forever and always your Momma, Avery, Dylan and Dad. x

Our Laura, forever 19, Love Mum and Dad. x

Joseph, 7 eskimo kisses to the moon and back and beyond. See you soon, my love. x

Dale Baker, aged 25. Missed and loved by all family and friends. x

I pray to God you are healed baby girl, but the day you didn't wake up is the day my world slipped away. Momma can't wait to see you again. In loving memory of Ava Rae Rose, 3-1-11 – 10-8-16.

Kevin Alan Mapes, aged 16. 8-31-01 – 3-2-18. Our contagious power ranger hero. We love and miss you so much. Our family chain is broken, we love you forever. Love Mom and Dad. x

Samuel David McClean Morton, 31-1-86 – 16-3-16, 30 years old. Forever in our hearts. x

Nicole Julianne Zaia, 18-9-78 – 5-6-10. Thank you for teaching us how to love. Unforgettable in life and forever missed. If only we knew then what we know now. Love Mum, Dad, Simone, Renee and all that knew her.

Clare Rachel Jeanes, 8-12-82 – 9-4-99, just 16 years old. A day that will live with us forever, miss you so much. Love Mum, Dad, Fiona and Jessica. x

Amy, my daughter, passed away 26-11-11. We miss her greatly. Dad. x

Nathan Daniel William LeBlanc, 5-15-11 – 2-29-16. Forever loved, forever missed, forever in our hearts. Until we find each other again little man. Love Mum, Dad and your little B.

Shaun Tyler Armes, 11-14-95 – 11-25-97. Son we love and miss you so very much, love you forever. Dad, Mum, Kody, Kaylee and little nephew, Tyler.

173

Jerome A.R. Beattie, 6-10-75 – 21-7-14, aged 38. Loving you always, Mum, Markus and family.

Zakary Durdahl, 25, dearly loved and always missed. Never will you be forgotten by your family. Love Teresa and your baby girl, Lucy.

Addison Cook, aged 8, you will always be our sunshine. x

Aaron Wayne Battle, age 16, 1990-2007. I love you forever. X

Missing you always Nathan Scott, aged 13. Amber. x

Jack Savelle, aged 5, 2-18-12 – 5-31-17. He displayed joy and unconditional love. We will see you soon sweet boy. X

Zachary Chase Godbout, forever 8. Born 4-8-02 – 24-4-11. You are my sunshine and I miss you. x